Art and Architecture

Suzanne Gonzales (signature)
July 13, 2002
Marfa, Texas

Art and Architecture

A Symposium Hosted by
The Chinati Foundation, Marfa, Texas,
on April 25 and 26, 1998

WITH LECTURES BY
James Ackerman
Michael Benedikt
Frank Gehry
Jacques Herzog
Roni Horn
Robert Irwin
Claes Oldenburg and
Coosje van Bruggen
MODERATOR
William F. Stern

Library of Congress Card Number 00-100749
ISBN 0-9673186-1-0

First Edition

The Chinati Foundation/La Fundación Chinati
1 Cavalry Row, P.O. Box 1135
Marfa, Texas 79843

CONTENTS

INTRODUCTION

William F. Stern

From the moment Chinati Foundation Director Marianne Stocke-brand suggested a symposium on art and architecture be held at the foundation, the idea seemed absolutely right. More than a decade before, having completed his installation for the Chinati Foundation in Marfa, Donald Judd had set the framework for an ongoing dialogue about art and architecture. In a place where contemporary ideas of both art and architecture are unusually combined, there was a clear basis for assembling a group of artists, architects, and scholars to join in a discussion.

Donald Judd's project in Marfa, as much as any work of its time, blurs the distinctions between what we call art and what we define as architecture. As a sculptor, Donald Judd had definite opinions about architecture. He decried imitation and had a low opinion of building that paraded itself in the guise of architecture when the building did not merit the distinction of the term. In architecture Judd sought the same degree of purity, unencumbered by style, that he sought in his art. At Chinati he directly fulfilled his beliefs by performing both the tasks of architect and artist. Taking on the direct role of the architect, he refashioned existing buildings, remnants of the U.S. Army's Fort D.A. Russell. In his introduction to the 1987 catalogue that documented the installation at Chinati he stated:

Most of the art was made for the existing buildings, which were dilapidated. The buildings were adjusted to the art as much as possible. New ones would have been better. Nevertheless, reworking the old buildings, I've turned them into architecture.

Among the buildings converted were two warehouses that had formerly been used by the Army for artillery storage. As Judd found them in the 1970s, the two artillery sheds were flat-roofed, enclosed warehouses, more building than architecture, ill-suited to the installation of one hundred mill aluminum pieces. To illuminate the interior spaces, Judd opened the long side walls with expanses of glass set within the existing reinforced concrete frame. The flat roof of each building was then covered with a prominent galvanized steel barrel, reminiscent of the neighboring agricultural or industrial sheds. A close examination of the mill aluminum pieces inside the artillery sheds reveals concerns that are as much sculptural as architectural. The very fact that these pieces are fabricated through a manufactured process, much as parts of a building are manufactured, aligns them with the precision associated with architecture. Like an architect, Judd the sculptor closely monitored the manufactured product, perfecting its joinery, as evidenced in the discreet fastening together of the aluminum plates. Even so, the mill aluminum pieces are a product of a sculptural investigation, displayed and seen within the architectural context of the artillery sheds and the natural context of landscape and light.

The two artillery sheds are only part of a larger ensemble of art and architecture. Below the sheds Judd installed the monumental concrete pieces, stretching across the plain in a composition that relates as much to the landscape as to the existing Fort Russell buildings. The nearby Arena building was modified as a place for gatherings and feasts, and the barracks buildings are used as offices, residences, and exhibition spaces. Donald Judd believed in the work of other artists with the same conviction as his own, and both during his lifetime and after, their work has been installed alongside his own. Installations of work by Roni Horn, Ilya Kabakov, and Carl Andre, among others, occupy a number of the barracks buildings; a major work of Dan Flavin designed specifically for six of the barracks buildings will open in 2000. Claes Oldenburg and Coosje van Bruggen's *Monument to the Last Horse* sits prominently among the dry grasses above the barracks. A Richard Long sculpture of stones laid out in a circle is sited just outside the Arena building, inside are two works by sculptor David Rabinowitch. A large collection of sculpture by John Chamberlain occupies the former wool and mohair warehouse in town.

*

In the second half of the twentieth century the relationship between art and architecture more often than not has been far from symbiotic. A traditional melding of painting, sculpture, and architecture was evident in ancient times, flourished in the Renaissance, and remained apparent even well into the early twentieth century; but it has changed in our own modern era. While architects and artists (in this case visual artists) share common affinities, their education, training, and product are more often than not quite different. Even so, these differences have not kept individuals from joining and crossing over into territory claimed by others.

To clarify the issues facing contemporary artists and architects, four artists, two architects, and two scholars were given the opportunity to engage in a dialogue through a presentation of their ideas, philosophies, and work. They were chosen because each approaches his or her work from a point of inclusion, and each could speak about experiences of collaboration. Specifically, the two architects presenting, Frank Gehry and Jacques Herzog, acknowledge influences from the artists they know and work with, either through collaborative involvement or through friendship and association. The artists Claes Oldenburg and Coosje van Bruggen have worked with architects (Frank Gehry at the Chiat/Day advertising building in Venice, California), but more often they have worked in the context of architecture and the city as a presence or a background. Likewise, Robert Irwin's work is often set within the environment of building or the topography of place, such as his recently completed garden at the Getty Center in Los Angeles. Roni Horn, whose work was admired and collected by Judd, acknowledges through her sculpture, photographs, writing, and site-specific pieces a keen awareness and relationship to building, place, and landscape. The Harvard art historian James Ackerman set an historical context for the dialogue, and Michael Benedikt, an architectural critic and writer on emerging technologies in the computer age, posed questions about art and architecture moving towards the future.

All of this took place over two days in the former Ice Plant, a metal shed building in the town of Marfa, Texas, not far from Judd's Chinati Foundation. Marfa is not an easy place to get to, so it was a surprise that within a few weeks of its formal announcement the symposium was fully subscribed with over six hundred in attendance. Perhaps the attraction was as much the place as the subject. Through the whole event, there was an overwhelming sense of the presence of Donald Judd's nearby installation. Few twentieth-century artists or architects have so skillfully combined disciplines; establishing, if nothing else, an immediate point of reference. As a voluminous writer and critic in his own right, Judd might be said to have instigated this discussion by provoking or inspiring a dialogue that comes out of the spirit of the place he found and shaped. While one could draw conclusions from the discussions, it was the visual presentation of work, and enunciation of countless ideas and positions that really sustained the symposium. The audience, gathered from all parts of the country and distant places from around the world, was brought together for a moment of concentration, only interrupted by the occasional rumble of a passing freight train. And between sessions, outside the darkness of the Ice Plant, in the bright sunlight of Southwest Texas, convivial conversations and debates could be heard.

What follows is the documentation of those presentations, a commentary on the potentials for art and architecture at the end of the twentieth century. From this remote corner of America, the place Donald Judd found and built upon, one senses that the dialogue will continue well into the future, with Judd's work at the Chinati Foundation serving as a point of reference, a springboard for the larger ideas he engendered.

THE FOLLOWING SYMPOSIUM LECTURES
ARE REPRINTED IN THE SEQUENCE IN WHICH
THEY WERE DELIVERED.
THEY WERE CONCEIVED AS SLIDE LECTURES
BUT THE NUMBER OF SLIDES PRESENTED
WAS REDUCED FOR THE PUBLICATION.

Unless otherwise noted,
the images accompanying the texts
represent work created
by the respective speaker.

ON SCULPTURE IN THE CONTEXT
OF ARCHITECTURE

James Ackerman

The theme of "Art and Architecture" scared me when I was invited to say something about it; it seemed uncontrollable. After some false starts, I thought to go to the library to look for writings of Donald Judd, guessing that they might provide some clue. They did; there are at least four short essays from different times entitled "Art and Architecture," and they started my ball rolling. They are far from representing Judd's best critical writing, being for the most part fulminations against the commercialism of contemporary architecture since Louis Kahn, but they do offer some starting positions for discussing the potentialities and agonies of placing sculpture in public architectural settings.

Judd was at war with the architecture in which his work might be placed. First of all, because architecture is loaded with meaning—the ideological messages of patrons, the ambitions of the architect, and the demands of its functions. Secondly, architecture forms the space around it, and if sculpture is also to be allowed to determine space, then it is likely to be in conflict with that of architecture; and finally, Judd saw architecture as the slave of commerce, and particularly in the post 1960s world; and in its surrender of autonomy, as having abandoned urbane amenities and social interchange in favor of the strip that destroys the city center.

I imagine that these propositions would be shared by the majority of non-figurative sculptors today, and especially those whose work, like Judd's, has itself many of the characteristics of architecture. Much sculpture in the 1960s broke away from or parodied that tradition and redefined the nature of sculptural space. Some sculptors and conceptual artists expressed the antagonism toward architecture by an effort to trash it: for example, Christo, who has completely concealed buildings with wrappings, or Matta-Clark, who has sawed buildings in half.

I propose to trace historically some of the steps by which artists were impelled into this adversarial position, starting with the revival of the classical tradition of monuments in public spaces in the Renaissance. I shall exclude observations on sculptural work that is applied to architecture in the form of relief or freestanding figures, because it is essentially a non-issue in twentieth-century associations of art and architecture.

Judd associated the classical tradition of public sculpture with the monolithic monument placed in an open space that is formed by an architectural environment. What preoccupied him was the way in which the meaning communicated by the architecture and its setting demands a kind of sculpture that would complement or be subordinated to building.

While it is true that artists through the nineteenth century were motivated by the tradition of the public monument requiring monolithic solutions on elevated architectural supports—usually placed in positions determined by the built environment—they were not restricted to echoing the message communicated by architecture. The equestrian statue of Colleoni in Venice, erected in the later fifteenth century to celebrate a victorious mercenary in the pay of the Republic, is placed on a square dominated by a monastic church and a charitable confraternity, the School of St. Mark. The piazza, or *campo* as the Venetians call it, is irregular in form, so the statue could not be centered, but its axis is determined by the buildings; in the depiction of the piazza by Canaletto the space is shown as substantially more regular than it

ANDREA VERROCCHIO, *Colleoni*, 1479/88; Campo San Zanipolo, Venice, Italy.
ANTONIO CANALE (Canaletto), *Campo San Zanipolo*, 1726, oil on canvas.

is, and the statue is moved and subordinated to the architecture.
Both the confraternity and the church of San Zanipolo (dialect ren-
dition of Ss. Giovanni and Paolo) were powerful in the society, but
they sought to convey messages quite distinct from that of the statue, which is relevant to Judd's concern about how the meaning of
an architectural context impinges on whatever art is placed in it.
Yet here, though the buildings have one meaning and the statue
another, it would be naive to claim that there was no connection
between military victories of the memorialized captain and the
interests of the church and the fraternity.

The very high base of the statue not only sets it off physically
and conceptually from the ground of human action, but helps it to
confront the scale of the buildings and the open space. These
advantages kept sculptors for the ensuing five hundred years from
daring to do without bases. I'm sure most visitors to the site can

GIANLORENZO BERNINI, *Four Rivers Fountain,* 1651;
Piazza Navona, Rome, Italy.

recall the statue better than the buildings, maybe because most of
us remember figurative sculpture better than architecture.

Bernini, one of the few pre-modern sculptors whom Judd
respected, also dealt powerfully with the weight of architectural
meaning in his Roman fountains. The *Four Rivers Fountain* is centered in the Piazza Navona, an oblong public space with one
curved end, the shape of which corresponds to the ancient circus,
or chariot racetrack, that lies beneath it. Circuses normally did
not have such central monuments in the ancient world, but rather
obelisks or columns at the ends to mark or symbolize the points at
which the contestants turned, and this partially explains Bernini's
choice of an Egyptian obelisk as the center of his composition. The
square is bordered by houses and elegant palaces and, near the
center, looming above the fountain, the two-towered church of St.
Agnese designed by Francesco Borromini, who had started his

SCULPTURE IN THE CONTEXT OF ARCHITECTURE

career as an assistant to Bernini at St. Peter. St. Agnese was tough competition, but Bernini more than held his own with an intensely theatrical choreography of allegorical human and animal figures representing the great rivers of four continents, and a fictive rocky mound and cave. Apart from the obelisk, the theme of Bernini's fountain did not supplement that of the church or of the pre-existing domestic buildings, but rather celebrated the abundance of water itself. Also, in that the figures represent four continents, there is an implication of Rome's—that is, the Church's—universal dominion. Bernini overcame the monolithic stasis of preceding public sculpture with the openness of his monument; space passes through it amidst the rocks, and the figures gesture out into the enveloping air, making the ensemble more a performance than a statue. It activates the entire great space of the piazza. Most fountains, since they have to hold water, escape the problem of the base, but the problem of the basin is no less challenging. Bernini resolved it in a number of ingenious ways in his Roman fountains, not the least in his decision to transform one into a boat drifting through a square (the *Baraccia* in the Piazza di Spagna).

No artist was as inventive and as liberated from the classical tradition as Bernini for the ensuing two centuries. A turning point to a new relationship between monumental sculpture and its urban or natural environment seems to me to come with Rodin's crisis over the installation of his *Burghers of Calais*, started in 1884. His charge was to memorialize the six heroic citizens who gave themselves up as hostages to save their fellow townspeople during a siege by the British in the fourteenth century. In this case, the environment itself was in flux, the demolition of the old defensive perimeter of the town had left a lot of empty space on the periphery, and the monument commission, perhaps because the abjectness of Rodin's group did not conform to its view of a heroizing monument, chose a site away from the town center, between a new

CALAIS. – Le Jardin Richelieu et le Monument des Bourgeois.

AUGUSTE RODIN, *The Burghers of Calais,* 1895, bronze;
initial installation in Calais, France (postcard).

post office and a public garden. The classical tradition had pro-
gressively abandoned tragedy and pain since the Hellenistic era of
the *Laocoön* and the *Pergamon Altar*, and the dramatic intensity of
Rodin's group did not sit particularly well with the town.

Rodin's first response was to raise the figures on the expected
tall podium, with somewhat classical moldings and projecting
lumps reminiscent of the Roman Rostra. He wrote at the time "The
socle is triumphal and recalls a triumphal arch," and this accorded
with the desire of the town commission to have the work elevated
on a podium. In 1912, he wrote of his attraction to the Verrocchio
equestrian monument because of its height, which he estimated at
five meters, and the proximity of the walls of neighboring church-
es (there is in fact only one church), and "the architecture of the
group has a grandeur that I cannot emphasize enough."

Rodin set to work in the late 1880s and early 1890s on the indi-

The Burghers of Calais, installation in Calais in the 1920s (postcard).

vidual figures, not focusing much on the ensemble and, when they were nearing completion, he was still undecided about how they should be distributed.

When the town had sufficiently recovered from the deep depression of the latter 1880s, the group was finally installed, in 1895, on a high podium designed by a local neo-classical architect. But already two years earlier, Rodin had expressed in a letter the idea of placing the group directly on the pavement of the square, an ambition to which he returned over a decade later, saying that he had wanted "to emphasize the effect still more...to fix my statues one behind the other on the stones of the *Place*, before the Town Hall of Calais, like a living chaplet of suffering and of sacrifice." He told Roger Fry that the monument "hangs together by its dramatic, but not its physical unity." The ground-level solution would have brought them right into the space of the viewer and intensified interaction with their tragic, expressionistic faces, movements, and gestures. Several writers on Rodin, including Rilke, reported this solution (without revealing that it had not been his preference from the start), but it was not Rodin's last word; in 1913, preparing for an installation of a replica by the Houses of Parliament in London, he placed casts of the group on a five meter high wooden platform built in his garden to study the problem. His incapacity to select between the two options was symptomatic of one of the agonies of modernism: whether or not to reject the support of tradition.

As Rodin's reputation grew, even Calais had second thoughts and reinstalled the *Burghers* in the early 1920s on a low base before the Town Hall, the site favored by the artist all along.

Rodin's thoughts about placing the figures on the ground represent one of the most radical and influential steps in the transition to the modern era, first because it abandoned at the same time monumentality and the monolithic, permitting the full opening of the work to the ambient space, which was that of the observer, and second because it gave sculpture an autonomy and a capacity to control its environment.

Its significance was to be grasped by Brancusi in his outdoor pieces, which are all set on the ground, and even more obviously by Giacometti, in his series of walking men, which evolved conceptually into the category of public sculpture in his *Piazza*, a virtual square given its character by the anonymous wraiths that stride through it with determination along paths controlled by its edges. Here Giacometti is bringing the public space into his sculpture while Rodin was attempting the opposite in conflicting ways, so *Piazza* is not at the kernel of this discussion, but it cannot be overlooked. It constitutes a critique of the issue.

The twentieth-century architects that Judd singled out for praise were Frank Lloyd Wright, Le Corbusier and Louis Kahn. I do not recall in the work of any of these admirable architects a readi-

ALBERTO GIACOMETTI, *Piazza*, 1948/49, bronze.

ness to collaborate with or even to accept sculptors as equal partners. Le Corbusier did his own monumental sculpture and even
that rarely, as in the *Open Hand* in Chandigarh, a sign of the recon-
ciliation of all fractions that ironically never was put in place due
to political conflict. Wright installed a neutral and subordinate
figure—significantly a Muse of Architecture—of his own design in
the garden at Taliesin East, and I can't remember any work coordi-
nated with a Kahn building. I think all three of these architects
thought about their buildings as having characteristics of sculpture. They did not, like the early modernist Adolf Loos, oppose
ornament and enrichment, but they wanted to and were capable of
giving sculptural values to their designs. The standoff has worked
in both directions, with the difference that architects can keep
sculptors out of their field of vision, while sculptors have no leverage to affect architecture aside from doing it themselves.

The classical tradition had long succeeded in representing the ideology of political and social power in such a way that sculpture and architecture could be joined to reinforce the message; during the nineteenth century and up to the realization of the sculptures by Paul Manship at Rockefeller Center in New York, and the several venues of the work of Carl Milles, the tranquilizing content and decorative finesse of public sculpture had assured its comradely incorporation into architecture. This accommodation was hard to maintain in the context of modernist architecture.

Mies van der Rohe's inclusion of a dancing figure by Georg Kolbe in the Barcelona Pavilion of 1929 was exceptional; the fact that the building was an exhibition structure without a specific function made it easier; in retrospect, as the late Robin Evans pointed out, it probably was intended to carry the urgent political message that the Germany of the Weimar Republic, unaware that it was on the eve of its erasure by the Nazis, was no longer a threat to Europe. Prophetically, the Kolbe sculpture was called *Evening*. The inaugural speech by the German minister of culture was paraphrased:

> Here you see the spirit of the new Germany: simplicity and clarity of means and intentions all open to the wind, as well as to freedom—it goes straight to our hearts. A work made of honesty, without pride. Here is the peaceful house of an appeased Germany!

In postwar America, government again intervened in the relationship of art to architecture; many federal and state commissions mandated two percent set-asides for art; the choice of artist was not necessarily the responsibility of the architect; a variety of selection processes were employed. Institutions also set aside funds in the same spirit. Alexander Calder was commissioned by M.I.T. to place a steel "stabile" in the piazza before the new Green

MIES VAN DER ROHE, German Pavilion for the 1929 Exposition
with a sculpture by Georg Kolbe; Barcelona, Spain.

Building, by I.M. Pei. (I served on the panel that recommended the
artist after unsuccessfully urging Jean Arp to take on the task; his
health was too poor to permit him to consider the project. I guess
he would have found the grand scale required by the setting
uncongenial to his approach.) Calder's *Grande Voile* in sheet steel
definitely displaces the classical dependence on the base and on
monolithic forms. It holds its own in a space dominated by the
building. It differs radically from later non-figurative art in its ges-
tural, biomorphic character, derived from Cubism and to some
extent from Surrealism. Yet it does not clash with the building. It
is a truly successful example of public art in an architectural environment, though the success may be due to its lack of challenge
and profundity. Calder was a pioneer in the employment of bolted
and riveted sheet steel; his use of industrial technology was conge-
nial to M.I.T., and encouraged younger artists to follow suit.

Judd's texts raise the question of the potential difference between monumental sculpture and public sculpture: a monument celebrates something; it refers to an existence outside itself; a public work is one in a public space that doesn't necessarily represent an intention to do so. But we should be cautious about the distinction: is it really possible to design an intervention in a public space that, intentionally or not, doesn't celebrate anything?

Is the expression of an ideology, which by definition is not consciously held by the maker or the patron, less charged with meaning than a triumphal arch or an allegory of peace? The issue might be raised by Judd's 1977 riverside work in Münster; two concrete rings establish in their material, concrete, and their geometry, both a harmony with and a contrast to the flatness of the river and the gentle undulations of the natural landscape. As in a similar composition in the private garden of Joseph Pulitzer in St. Louis, the slope of the ground establishes the angle of one square and the horizon, or the river surface, of the other. I read this as celebrating the meeting of human culture, which produced geometry and concrete, and nature (which in this case is superficially tamed by culture). Whether or not this was what Judd had in mind in composing the work is not at issue, as it could legitimately be in a critique of Rodin's *Burghers*.

I have more license to arrive at this interpretation than I would in the case of one of the more numerous pieces of Judd designed to be exhibited in a gallery space. In such a space the environment is not a factor, unless it happens to be intrusive. So a non-figurative work of this kind can be seen primarily in respect to its intrinsic form, materials, and color. This is why Judd repeatedly sought to have his work shown in a neutral and permanent environment, preferably one like the indoor ones at Marfa, over which he had maximum control. Most photographs of Judd's work in gallery spaces are made so that they convey virtually nothing of the environment. In such works, Judd came as near as anyone in our time

DONALD JUDD, untitled, 1977, concrete; Münster, Germany.

DONALD JUDD, untitled, 1970, stainless steel and plexiglas.

to achieving distance from expression. If there is any reference to the world outside of art, it is to architecture, in its floor and walls assembled from rectilinear planes.

Postmodern criticism has attempted to distance the artist from the viewer. What the artist intended to communicate, indeed whether he or she intended to communicate, is no longer relevant. What the viewer, in turn, says or thinks about a work is in some scenarios also irrelevant and in others unrestrained from whatever creative flights may be inspired in the presence of the work. We owe much to postmodern approaches, but for all their benefits to criticism, interpretation, and the intellectual climate, they cannot in the long run override the urge of viewers to enter into a dialog with works of art. We are genetically disposed to interact with things in the outer world.

RICHARD SERRA, *Tilted Arc,* 1981, Cor-ten steel;
Federal Plaza, New York City (destroyed).

The high-water mark of the conflict of art and architecture was reached by Richard Serra's *Tilted Arc,* commissioned by the General Services Administration for Federal Plaza in New York City. The plaza is bordered by some innocuous classical buildings with columnar façades, but the assigned site is dominated by a multi-storied structure faced with the crude patterned cladding of a cheap motel. The concentric design of the plaza pavement, probably designed by the same architect, is also feebly patterned in a way that defies accommodation by any conceivable work of art. Serra's response was not merely to ignore the setting but to assault it with a powerful work that, while it had to be received only on its own terms, also acknowledged the setting in an adversarial way, as was clear in his written defense of the project. The public response was violently negative; Serra's work was vandalized and ultimately removed and destroyed (in 1989) by the agency that had commissioned and financed it, after a lawsuit that ended in a judgment that the property rights of the government supersede the expressive rights of the maker, that First Amendment protection did not apply.

Two issues came together in this debacle. Public distaste for unfamiliar and shocking artistic expression, which is intensified when expression is domineering, and public response to the incompatibility of the work of art with its environment, which amounted in the case of *Tilted Arc* to impeding easy access to and from the building.

But the outcome cannot simply be attributed to philistinism, because another difficult and unfamiliar public work of the same period, the Vietnam Veterans' Memorial in Washington, while it initially met vigorous opposition, was in a surprisingly short time accepted and admired.

It is a monument in the tradition of war memorials with respect to function, but strikingly different from the tradition in form. Ironically, the form is indebted to a work by Serra. Above all, it does not belong in the category of sculpture in architecture because it is undeniably sculpture *and* architecture. It is the only memorial monument of our time that I could think of that abandons an erect configuration and any exaltation of victory or noble defeat.

The issue of competition with the imposing architectural monuments around it does not arise, although its angles point directly toward the Lincoln Memorial on the west, which is reflected on its polished granite surfaces, and the Washington Monument on the east. Although the surrounding site is charged with grand gleaming white shrines, this is black, and below ground level in its own subterrestrial space, suggesting the grave. Apart from this, its message is conveyed primarily in its medium, names engraved on granite. We see that these men and women died not, as in Rodin's monument, for their countrymen, not for the honor of their country,

Tilted Arc, aerial view.

but in thousands of individual tragedies within a great national tragedy. If this constitutes a narrative, it is more one of these names than of figuration in the design.

The issue, which may be central to much of the discourse in this volume, is whether in our time it is possible for art and architecture to function interactively. Was Judd right to question whether non-referential sculpture can be public in the traditional sense of communicating something of the public ideology or belief, and whether it could be reinforced by an architecture that is designed with a cognate intention? Or, is our market-dominated culture so lacking in a common belief that public sculpture can only comment on the lack, in the sense that much of the work of Claes Oldenburg has done, in ironically sustaining the tradition of the monolithic monument? Is there any option between the possibility of a non-narrative sculpture that is in conflict with its architectural surrounding in the way of *Tilted Arc*, and one that perpetuates the classical tradition of the talking monument?

COLLABORATIONS WITH ARTISTS, MUSEUM PROJECTS, AND OUR FIRST BUILDING IN AMERICA

Jacques Herzog

In three separate parts I will try to approach the subject of art and architecture as part of our daily practice. In the first part I'll mention a few collaborations we've had with artists to date, in the second part I'd like to present museum projects and built museums, and in the third part I'd like to present our first building in this country, the recently finished Dominus Winery.

Over the years we've come to understand more and more that artists shouldn't do architecture and architects shouldn't do art. I hope we can talk about that later. We have also understood that it's very important to fuse these things, to bring these things together. In many projects we came to a point where we found it absolutely important and necessary to involve an artist to make the project better. This involvement was not to have decoration, or to add a piece that would make the project nicer, although this could also be a possibility. We wanted more of a collaboration, to have the artist be a part of the team, and we've been lucky to have two artists living in Basel, Helmut Federle and Rémy Zaugg. They have been friends for a very long time, even before we studied architecture, so it was natural for us to collaborate with them, to look at the world through the eyes of an artist as well. For instance, both of these artists were critiquing museum buildings even before I started looking at museums, so any debate about museums is something about which we have been familiar since very early on, and it has been a serious concern, not just as an architectural issue.

We've been lucky in another way, in that Basel is a city of art with fantastic museums. It's a city where contemporary art has always been shown at very early moments in artists' careers. For example, I saw Donald Judd's drawings in the early 1970s at the Kunstmuseum in Basel and they impressed me by their lack of decoration and by the direct way they communicated the artist's idea. Another important artist was Joseph Beuys, who played an important role in a very special way. When we left university in the mid-1970s we had almost no work, but we really wanted to express ourselves creatively, so we accepted work from a carnival group in Basel. Basel Carnival has an important and long tradition. We did the costumes and masks for this group for many years. After a while we became bored because Carnival is basically about irony and treating subjects polemically; it's never really about taking a political subject and making the whole performance on the street the main event. So sometime between 1976 and 1978, I don't remember exactly when, the city of Basel bought *Feuerstätte I*, an important piece by Beuys. Of course the purchase was a big political issue, the piece cost $300,000 at the time. The city bought it, and that became a main subject at Carnival. Many groups treated the subject in their typical, ironic way. We wanted to turn the whole event into an artist's performance, including Beuys and his work. He agreed to work together with us, and he designed a performance on which we assisted him. This was, in a way, our first collaboration with an artist.

What we did in fact was copy the sculpture *Feuerstätte I*, and the Carnival group performing the piece carried these iron and copper sticks on the streets for three days. They were dressed in Beuys's felt suits and we made gold masks for the whole group of sixty people. By the end of those three days, this sculptural copy of *Feuerstätte I* became a different thing. By being carried through the

JOSEPH BEUYS, *Feuerstätte 2*; Basel, Switzerland.

streets, it became a different sculpture. This sculpture became *Feuerstätte II*, which is now on display in the Gegenwartsmuseum (museum of contemporary art) in Basel. This experience was very important to us because it allowed us to learn more about Beuys's world, which was quite a shock and quite different from our experiences at the ETH school in Zürich, where we studied under Aldo Rossi. So after Carnival we were familiar not only with the very southern world of Aldo Rossi, but also with the northern, romantic world of Beuys. This became very important in that Beuys used materials in a totally new and unexpected way.

Rémy Zaugg is the artist with whom we've collaborated most; we always have one or two projects that we are working on with him. The idea is to truly examine all the different possible ways of working with someone, from very small-scale to urban designs. What we've learned from our collaboration with Rémy is that the

Master Plan for the University of Burgundy, Dijon, France; project 1989/90.
Campus before Herzog and de Meuron's intervention.

artists in whom we're most interested are very strong conceptually and their work is not solely concerned with aesthetic attributes. So Rémy's thinking is what we are interested in; it is a different view on things.

This shows the campus of the university in Dijon, France. Rémy looks at the world, at this campus, as if it was a surface of a painting. He sees things from such a different angle. This is the thing which fascinates us and it remains interesting in totally different projects as well. The case in Dijon was reversed, here the artist came to us and asked us to collaborate, because he was commissioned to do a museum on the campus. It's a campus that was built in the 1960s and again in the 1980s, when the Socialists were powerful. There was a lot of money to do many buildings, including this art museum. Rémy needed an architect so he contacted us. The first thing we needed to do was a master plan, because we didn't

Antipodes I, Student Housing, University of Burgundy;
project 1990, realized 1991/92.

know where to put the museum. We analyzed this campus, which
has a very strange structure with very powerful buildings from the
1960s; they are a kind of mixture between Perret and Le Corbusier;
other buildings in the background are more fuzzy. The whole
place seemed to be losing its integrity and urban quality, so the
master plan we did was very conceptual. We saw that the city of
Dijon has onion-like layers around its center. We wanted the campus to be part of the city, not just an isolated place. We tried to
change the campus to make it more permeable to the surrounding
neighborhood of the city. It somehow became a very didactic lesson to the people working there, and the communication with
these people became the most interesting thing about the project.
We often tried to turn existing structures into courtyard buildings; we then inserted them in layers to allow for connections of
the campus in these directions. The radical, almost schematic

graphic design of this plan demonstrates Rémy's role and his strong influence on this project. It illustrates the artist's way of speaking very clearly in very simple terms. Green for green areas between built areas, grey for existing and so on. What finally turned out to be so simple was quite difficult to achieve at the beginning. In the end we couldn't build the museum because the Socialists lost power and that was the end of many large projects in France. But we were able to build dormitories on the campus with very little money, just before the Socialists lost power. We could have done one building, a very long building which sort of stretched between two *allées*. And we integrated a new road on the campus and our master plan became an official plan, *the* master plan. The people from the university, in a very French tradition, called this new avenue *Avenue du 21e Siècle*: The Avenue of the Twenty-first Century. So this is part of the twenty-first century.

Another collaboration with artists came about in 1991 when we were invited to exhibit our work in the Swiss Pavilion at the Venice Bienale. We didn't want to do this show ourselves. We did the buildings, but we didn't want to do pieces which would explain or demonstrate these buildings, so we asked artists to take photographs of their choice of our buildings and to make the show. So it was not only our show, it was also the show of the four artists we invited: Balthasar Burkard, Hannah Villiger, Margherita Spiluttini, and Thomas Ruff. Hannah Villiger usually does portraits of her own body, based on Polaroids which she blows up. In this case she enlarged a Polaroid of one of our buildings. This is the first photograph that Thomas Ruff took of one of our buildings, and it was the beginning of a collaboration which continues today. We were interested in Thomas's work because at first glance it's very straightforward, but it becomes ambiguous as you study it in depth. We were also struck by the different groupings of his work, which reminded us of our own strategy of establishing several lines of work, separate strategies that can be worked on in par-

Ricola Storage Building, Laufen, Switzerland; project 1986, realized 1987.

allel. His lines include his portraits, his stars, his houses, his posters, and also his private collection of newspaper photography. This is a picture that Thomas took of Dijon; it has an almost sad aspect to it.

Thomas took new pictures of our buildings for a show at Peter Blum's gallery in New York. This photo of the Ricola storage building has this frontal view that reminded us very much of Thomas's portraits.

Another project is on a campus in Eberswalde, near Berlin. We were commissioned to do two buildings. We proposed adding these two buildings so that they would complete a square, which was one of the few that remains in the old city in Eberswalde, in the former East Germany. We decided to add these things like missing teeth in a mouth, not to find totally new shapes, but to invent a new urban type.

This is a seminar building and a library which is now under construction, which is in addition to the existing library. The existing building is in the typical style of the place; it's not really nice, but it has some character and atmosphere. We wanted to do something which was different, but at the same time have the structure reflect the character of the old architecture. This is the existing library and the new piece linked with the corridor. It is a very, very simple rectangular box, three floors, almost like stacks of books. There was no possibility to turn the library into a spatially interesting thing inside, which would have meant a higher space or a more public space for circulation—informal, unprogrammed space. That was a restriction we had to accept, so we radicalized this restriction and turned it into a kind of stack with a storage of books. In between the books, the readers and the students find their space with little windows and bands of glass on top, a structure a bit like we did at the Goetz Gallery. From the very beginning we were interested in having pictures all over the building, so as to totally mask the box. The box would be very simply shaped, but the

Seminar Building and Library for the Eberswalde Technical School,
Eberswalde, Germany; project 1994/95, realized 1996/97.
Façade collaboration with Thomas Ruff's archive photographs.

fact that it's totally tattooed would destroy a simple reading of this geometrically clear, clearly shaped building.

When we began we found a method for applying photographic pictures into the surface of concrete. We applied this technique for the first time in a sports center in France. It's a method which stops the concrete from drying in some areas, allowing us to wash it out very carefully so that any type of photo will appear. This allows us to use the stone surface of the concrete like photographic paper. The natural grain of the concrete and the grain of the photograph interfere with each other in very interesting ways; from further away the picture appears very much like a photograph, but the closer you come it turns out to be stone and the picture almost fades completely. So it's not like a Pop Art poster, its visible evidence is always changing. Once we discovered this technique, we knew this could be interesting for an artist like Thomas Ruff, who is very open to new ways of dealing with photography, so we asked him to work with us on the project in Eberswalde. Thomas has a collection of images known as his archive series. They are images that for some reason attract his attention; he finds them in magazines and newspapers and collects them and uses them later in his exhibitions. We thought that this collection would provide a fantastic resource from which to take pictures. Thomas agreed to work on the project and he made proposals of images to employ in covering the entire façade.

The images are in repetition horizontally, and changing vertically; they were images printed on concrete as well as on glass. The larger ones are glass bands and the smaller ones are concrete slabs. With daylight, when no light appears inside, the building looks homogeneous, like a monolithic block with images running around the building. Behind each small window is an individual table for reading, and the upper, wide bands is where daylight enters the interior of the building.

Using photography was very interesting politically and socially in this project, because the university is in the former East Germany and there was conjecture about some of Thomas's motives. Of course, Thomas played the political game very cleverly and he used charged images, including a skull, a *memento mori* image—a very traditional image for a library. He also used an image of people escaping from East Berlin in 1961, when the Russians were building the wall. We found that many people at the university and in the surrounding area still couldn't deal with the political content of these images, but as architects we were only interested in having images on the façade; we wanted to change, to totally destroy the purely geometrical shape of the box.

Another collaboration arose when the Pompidou Center asked us to do a show. This was clearly an occasion where we wished to do something with Rémy Zaugg. As you may know, Rémy curated a show of Alberto Giacometti at the Musée d'Art Moderne in Paris. It was one of the most brilliant shows we had ever seen, so we asked him to develop the concept for our show. Initially this may have sounded like a strange question, but he finally liked the idea very much.

Most architecture shows are like shows of artwork, just less good. We wanted to void this fact, and create something very powerful, something that expressed not an artistic power, but an architectural power, made even more powerful by the fact that it was done by an artist. We wanted to have everything in one space with no subdivisions and no inner walls. Rémy laid the material out on tables under glass, and he created a pattern reminiscent of a city plan. The tables with models atop them were slightly lower, so that the flatness of the installation became a major sculptural quality. The light expressed the same order, it was extremely bright. Upon entering the exhibition you were struck by the things that were really, as Rémy said, "brought to daylight." The projects were laid out chronologically, with no project given more or less hierarchical weight. We created interesting connections between the things that extended a bit over the tables. For example, the models of the Signal Boxes #1 and #2 were spatially related, almost as they would be in a city landscape. The chairs were normally arranged between the tables, a bit like in a library. The atmosphere was more that of a library or a study center than a show of pictures on a wall. We also installed some monitors showing videos about our work; these monitors were treated in the same way. We added some important pieces that artists had created about our work or which related in some way to how we think about the city or about perception, about similar issues.

There has been one other collaboration with Rémy, designing his studio. This was very tough because his work is about perception and it's very critical of museum spaces. You may know his very impressive and thick book entitled *Die List der Unschuld*, where he describes Donald Judd's sculpture of seven steel boxes and its posi-

Studio Rémy Zaugg, Mulhouse, France; project 1995, realized 1995/96.

tion in the Kuntmuseum Basel. The whole book is a lesson about the relationship between space and works of art. Doing this studio was a real test for us to show how a museum space should be, because even though it's a workspace, it still has the character of a space where art is viewed. We did a very simple scheme with two roofs and two canopies. One canopy relates to this wall, creating a simple space outside, and the other almost opens the studio to the garden, which was landscaped by Rémy himself. Basically he flattened out the whole garden and treated it like a painting. He made it flatter than flat, it's probably the flattest spot on the planet.

We did something with this building that we are trying to do in quite a few current projects—we treated the building like a natural object. We collected rainwater on the roof and the water just falls down, as if coming off a rock or off your own head as you walk through the rain. This water created interesting paintings on the

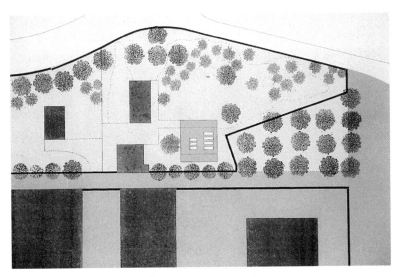

Studio Rémy Zaugg. Site plan.

outside, reminiscent of Morris Louis. Of course this wasn't done intentionally, it should only be rainwater and algae running down the wall, but the fact that this other substance became visible was alarming. We found out that the factory close to Rémy's grounds had very old technology and it was pollution from the factory that became visible on the wall. It wasn't dangerous, but still we could see the consequence of this factory, and we understood why the property was so inexpensive. In the meantime they've stopped production and Rémy will be able to buy even more of this property for a good price! We decided finally to keep the water stains and to let it be part of the weathering and aging process of the building. In the evening other sections of the building reveal themselves, there's storage and a place to write. There is more production space and also a space for presentation. The plan shows the existing buildings, including the villa which belonged to the former owner of the factory, the huge factory buildings behind, and the new studio. The skylights on top of the studio are arranged in a very simple way, I'll talk about that later. The layout is very simple, two studios, storage, and a bathroom.

This studio was a very important experience, especially in terms of natural light. It's like a full-scale model for one type of gallery we are doing for the Tate Gallery at Bankside. Daylight enters from the side, from floor to ceiling. The skylights are cut into the ceiling in simple rectangular forms, inserted with etched glass slabs flush with the ceiling. The advantage of this is that it's technically very simple and it creates a very homogeneous spatial quality. The ceiling has the same material quality as the walls, so you don't get the feeling that the ceiling flies away from the room. And yet it's very bright and it's very relaxed and generous. For this studio the technical background is very simple, almost primitive. And the roof and the floor are basically the same structure, which then opens the pavilion to the garden.

The next group of things I'd like to talk about are museums. First, the Goetz Gallery in Munich, a private collection of contemporary art which is run a bit like a Kunsthalle. The public can visit by appointment and the shows change about every six months. This is an elevation from the street side and from the garden. You can see at first sight how the building works as a simple box, but in fact it has two stories with the lower floor partly sunken in the garden. This is because we could not make the building higher and we needed to find a way to have two equally important floors. So we developed the idea of sinking the building into the ground. It's a very simple geometry but it has a complex spatial system. It is one piece with two tunnel-like openings which cut across. But it can be read as a structure standing on two socles, and it can also be understood as something more solid, situated between two light bands. The different appearances of the building become more evident with the change of light during the day as well as with the change

Gallery for a Private Collection of Modern Art, Goetz Collection, Munich, Germany; project 1989/90, realized 1991/92.

of seasons. It's certainly one of the best examples to show that many of our buildings deal with the issue of change, that they enhance the fact that light and seasons change all the time. The material we used is very pale birch plywood; we also planted birch trees as a landscape element. We increasingly worked on the combination between the plants of the garden, the landscape, and their relationship with the building and its materials. We also used etched glass and anodized aluminum so that with daylight, these three very different materials seem very close to each other. With the change of light they differentiate very clearly. As the light inside becomes stronger, the structure becomes more evident and begins to reveal other qualities not seen before. In some light conditions it resembles a lantern in the garden that, in this case, we've arranged in a very simple way.

The glass panels of this building appear in many different ways. It's slightly mirrored in areas, so that the building becomes a part of the garden, like a pond or a frozen section of the garden. When you are in the lower part of the building you don't have the feeling of being in the basement; you have the identical spatial feeling as the one you have on the upper floor. We wanted to create this homogeneous feeling because it's a small building. In a larger building it would be terrible to have created this claustrophobic atmosphere, but within a small building it's certainly an advantage, especially if you have two exhibitions by different artists, as neither would want to be in the lower part.

Inside one of the tubes which cuts through is a space that works as an entrance lobby or a little library. From there you go up one stair to the upper floor or down one stair to the lower gallery. This stairwell works like a part of the exhibition space, as Jeannie Goetz often starts her shows in the stairwell. This is how the spaces work, with these light glass bands on top and on the side, which bring daylight in. It's a very simple construction with two glass layers through which we can control the light, the shading, and the

Gallery for a Private Collection of Modern Art, Goetz Collection.
Stairwell with a work by Cindy Sherman.

use of energy. One advantage of the building is its very low-tech construction, it still allows for very subtle adjustments to climate control. We started the design by cutting the openings into the ceiling, in this case only for artificial light. Again, as in Rémy Zaugg's studio, the glass is flush with the ceiling and that's where we found the possibility to make the skylights larger and to have them work as places where daylight could enter the building.

The Goetz Studio was an important experience for us, and it allowed us to begin work on a larger scale. We wanted this type of gallery to be an important part of the new Tate Gallery at Bankside, which is now under construction. This huge brick building—which we always thought looked a bit like a brick mountain—is so large that it took a while to understand how to approach it, how to work with it in terms of architectural strategy. We decided to work with it and not against it, to use the advantages it has and to make a radical design that would make the existing things even more powerful. At first we disliked the chimney, but it clearly relates to St. Paul's Cathedral and we realized Sir Giles Scott's idea was clearly to establish this urban relationship. We didn't want to work against that, we wanted to intensify the urban aspect of the building. You can see how this building is established and why it wouldn't make sense to create new, more funny openings in the façade or to add an extraneous piece. It would fall apart or appear ridiculous, especially taking into account the incredible mass of the building. We needed a more subversive strategy. This shows how the building will look more or less, this is a 3-D picture, one of those glossy pictures produced by someone else. It is not really how we see the future building but it's one of these "political" images which helps to raise money for an architectural project. One of the major pieces of the building will be this glass beam we set atop, like a horizontal answer to the chimney. It forms a cross and it also balances the building in a new way.

The cross form is not just a sign with a symbolic meaning, like a Christian sign; it has to do with the existing structure of the building and with the way it will be accessible in the future. The building was originally designed to keep people away. Although as a power station it was attractive—especially this tower—at the same time it did everything to keep people away. Now we have to do the opposite, we have to do everything to welcome people and to bring them in. So we removed smaller additions to the building in order to create views of the city and to understand where the building is and how it stands on the ground. This may seem simple, but it wasn't so evident to work in such a straightforward way. The huge brick mass needed to be grounded, and to enhance that, we decided you would be able to enter the building complex from all sides— north, south, east, and west—again the cross. We also created a big ramp on the west side where you can go down to the lowest existing level of the building. The building turned out to be much

Tate Gallery of Modern Art, London, England; competition 1994, project 1995, realized 1995/2000. View from the north bank of the River Thames.

higher when we dug it out, and this full height allowed the experience of the whole building.

Here is an image of the former Turbine Hall and the level here is the actual pedestrian level outside. We decided to take all of that out, because there was more space below. The original level outside will be the ramp where visitors will enter the building. The galleries will be behind the former Boiler House. The whole building is so large that many people will use it just to walk through—either down the ramp or from the north to the River Thames—without even visiting the galleries. The main thing to decide on the inside was how to keep the Turbine Hall, which had already been conceived as a grand space. We kept that and tried to enhance it, to make it even higher and to expose the existing space, just as Rémy exposed our work to the viewer. It has an almost cathedral-like character due to the elongated shape of the existing windows. Truly this

Tate Gallery of Modern Art. Turbine Hall before intervention.
Ramp leading into the Turbine Hall.

will work as a major public space in London. The whole space is 160 meters long; it's reminiscent in scale to the Galleria in Milan. It's not only a public space, it's also a space in which art will be displayed. The platform links the north and south parts of the neighborhood. This is the ramp which leads people down into the Turbine Hall. In many ways the Turbine Hall corresponds to the Duveen Gallery in the existing Tate at Millbank, where contemporary art works extremely well within very strong, classical architecture. We often spoke about this with Nick Serota and we strongly hope to create possibilities for contemporary art in the Turbine Hall.

This shows a section through the Turbine Hall and the former Boiler House, where we will have galleries on three levels. On two lower levels will be the entrances, the mechanical plant, the auditorium and the restaurant. Missing from this plan is the third building layer, which is the switch house. Under the switch house

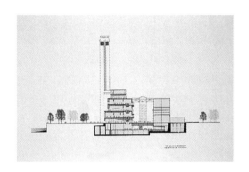

Tate Gallery of Modern Art. Cross section through building,
Boiler House with galleries on left, Turbine Hall on right.
Maquette showing façade of the galleries and concourses
facing the Turbine Hall.

are three huge oil tanks which, in a later phase, will be used as
spaces for contemporary art. So it's not just a museum that you
enter, but a whole world with a variety of different spaces. Once
you go down the ramp you can experience the building from different directions and discover totally different spaces. Bankside is
a model for a museum which offers many different typologies. It is
a heterotopic site for art and people in the twenty-first century.

This picture shows a maquette where we tested different
options for the new interior façade of the museum as seen from
the Turbine Hall. We were studying how these pieces will cut
through the steel structure and stand out, so you can see them
from a perspective view. The trusses, the columns are so thick that
they cannot be seen as a frontal view, so we had to find an element
which expresses the fact that it's a museum, but which also allows
people to have a view into the Turbine Hall once they exit an exhi-

bition space. These spaces are a kind of rest area, like little lounges within the gallery layout. The glass pieces are etched glass and transparent glass, they work as monitors providing information about shows in the building. People will walk down the ramp, enter the building and see these big glass monitors. It was very important for us to provide good orientation so that people don't feel lost in such a big building. As I said before, one gallery type has a similar skylight system as that which we developed for Rémy Zaugg. We did tests until it was technically and aesthetically as we wanted it to be. We think that the daylight and the artificial light which will come through the openings will provide a magic quality. People will have the impression that daylight filters in throughout the building, because there will almost always be daylight entering from the side in the galleries.

There is a dramatic change in scale as you walk through the galleries. Most of these rooms are five meters high, then suddenly you enter an area of double height, exposing the full height of the existing cathedral windows. These spaces are extremely high spaces, between ten and fourteen meters. Next to these big spaces visitors will also find more intimate spaces. So there is a whole range of spatial variety throughout the building.

Another big museum project we worked on was the expansion of the Museum of Modern Art in New York. This image shows how the new museum would have looked from Fifth Avenue into Fifty-fourth Street. In our plan, Fifty-fourth Street would have been as important as Fifty-third, because two entrances would lead visitors through the museum, including those people who would not necessarily want to visit the galleries. It's a strategy to open the museum to everyone, just as we proposed for Bankside. On the Fifty-fourth Street side the museum looked much more homogeneous than on the other side, but it would no longer have been a back façade, it would have been a new front. We decided to use all glazed façades with different surface qualities, slightly mirroring

Museum of Modern Art, New York City; competition 1997.
View from Fifth Avenue with the new curatorial tower overlooking the site.

glass and transparent glass. The garden is in the middle, so that literally wherever you went as a visitor it will always be around the garden. The new side of the museum would have been topped by a new tower, which we termed the curatorial tower. It started on Fifty-third Street and wrapped around the existing MoMA tower and then looked down onto the new side. The tower was not only a sign, it also contended with the change of function, with the way that research, conservation, and education will be major issues in the next century.

On the Fifty-third Street side there was a more heterogeneous character with the Johnson building, the Pelli building and our building standing in a row, all working as individual pieces, one next to the other. The tower looked very different from all sides. As it was a curatorial tower, it had different curatorial departments on different floors and each floor would have looked unique.

The garden and our concept were extremely simple. We had galleries on two floors plus the entrance floor, with all galleries around the garden, so that wherever you were you had a view of both the garden and the city. We wanted people to arrive and be able to take the stairs without having to confront these difficult escalators as they are now. So all that was gone from our plan. The plan shows how we wanted the lobby to be one space wrapping around the garden, while also functioning as a gallery. We took out one floor, so that the space is much higher, and we also made it larger on the side so that the garden literally extended into the entrance lobby. As in our strategy for Bankside, the garden would have been an existing quality, explored as a major element.

On the upper floor the space worked like a narrative, it led people through the entire site so that the rhythm of the building, and the rhythm of walking through it, combined with the rhythm of the collection. It wasn't just one big sequence of more or less elegant, bank-like spaces. A big space was to exist between Fifty-third and Fifty-fourth Streets, allowing for large scale shows. One final note on the tower: it was conceived by examining its geometric possibilities, while also taking into account zoning and air rights. It wasn't an invented shape, it was not "expressive" in an individualistic sense of the term, it was determined by the specificity of the place, like a plant in the forest. Working on this tower was an important and interesting starting point for H&deM to develop and discover new shapes and spaces.

A last museum project in this series is actually a private home and museum for Pam and Dick Kramlich, collectors of media art living in the Napa Valley. In this project we tried to figure out a way in which people could live in the house and live with video art at the same time. We are seeking to develop a non-classical type of gallery, without the need of rectangular, firm walls. The art will be shown in a building structure that flows, as opposed to a structure

Kramlich Residence and Video Collection, Oakville, California; project 1997/98, realized 1999/2000. Interior showing possible projection of videos on etched glass wall.

which separates things more traditionally. We developed wave-like walls which literally flow throughout the entire building. All of the walls, the outer walls as well as the inner, will be glass of varying material quality. All of the areas—bedrooms, living room, pool, library, entrance and galleries—will be in one sequence, so that every wall touches upon the realm of daily life of another area in the building.

We are working with a video artist to figure out how we can use these glass walls to project the videos. The building will work like a big screen, so that the art can be on the walls but there will also be a system of curtains which will run throughout the building, transforming the spaces into more protected or more intimate spaces. Here's a possibility with the video projected onto one of the inner walls. The façade here is just a very rough sketch, combined with furniture. This is what we're working on at the moment.

Dominus Winery, Yountville, California; project 1995, realized 1996/98.
View of interior.

The first building we did in America is a winery for Christian and Cherise Moueix, French winegrowers from Bordeaux who, since 1984, have been creating a California wine in Yountville called Dominus. Don't forget this name! It's an absolutely outstanding wine in an incredible landscape, so it was a big challenge for us to cope with these things in terms of the building. We tried to find a way to work in this landscape with all of its climatic concerns, but we also wanted in some way to address its cultural issues. We wanted to use stone in a new way, and we discovered the possibility of working with gabions, steel baskets which we filled with stones. We used both small and large stones, so that they remained loose. They're not bound with mortar in the traditional way, and the solid mass of the stones can absorb heat during the day and release heat on the cooler nights. This is ideal, especially for wineries, and it's something which is very old but it's been for-

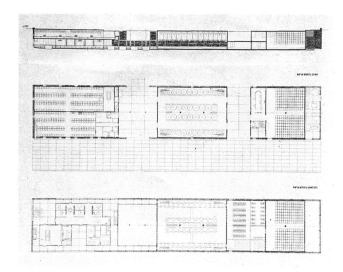

Dominus Winery. Plan.

gotten and has never been used in this country, where oil prices are very low.

The inner glass walls are sort of doing the opposite, they let the light in and illuminate the almost immaterial form of the stones. The landscape is gorgeous and because it's a very large building, we didn't want to create a structure which would totally compromise the landscape. That's why we found this dark, basalt stone. It's a volcanic material which in daylight almost vanishes in the landscape. It also vanishes in another way. It's inserted in the vineyard as in a text, where the lines of the vines are like written lines, and the building is placed so that it sits across this main axis. We created the building thinking about heat, light, and other elements that affect the winemaking process, but we also were intent on framing views in this fabulous landscape in a very special way. We created a big space which is a bit like in a Spanish hacienda.

This is the place where everything comes together, the owners, the tasters and the workers. It's a place where trucks and cars—everything—comes together.

In the plan you can see that the layout very simply has three units. From the main arch you can see in the middle the tank room, where the grapes are crushed. From there the grapes go to the barrel cellar, an elegant barrel cellar normally open to a few visitors. On the upper floor is the wine library, sitting atop of a second arch; it's not a public place, it's a place where people come together from the tank room and storage. The upper floor with offices sits atop of the barrel cellar, and the bridge-like pieces link the different units.

This image probably expresses best our intention to expose the stone with this archaic, heavy quality. At the same time, when you walk through, it changes and becomes something different, almost transparent. When we worked on the gabions we built mock-ups as we did for the Tate, to be really sure that these new methods would work. We needed to be sure that these big stones with gaps between them would let sunlight come in during the day and then at night release the light from inside. From some views the structure looks more archaic, as if the steel wires are strings holding the masonry together. Behind the stones are either concrete walls for better insulation, or glass walls for the offices and other public places. In some places, such as in the mechanical bay area, we have nothing behind.

In the morning and evening, when the sun hits the sides of the building the steel mesh reflects more of its own material quality. And the space between the galleries is very wide, so that the landscape filters into the building from all sides during the day. And finally at night the reverse happens, so that when daylight is gone the artificial light within becomes strongly visible.

Roni Horn

We have to start in the dark. I know you just had your lunch. I'm going to be your intermezzo.

The work over the years has ranged in many different idioms: visually very broad, virtually camouflaged by its own diversity. So you'll see photo-based installations, drawings, so-called sculpture or three-dimensional installations, and a collective work entitled *To Place*, which is an encyclopedia. Originally it was an encyclopedia that was based in the form of Plato's *Dialogues*. But I thought it over and this really isn't ambitious enough. So of course I went to the *Encyclopedia Brittanica* because of its episodic form, which I found extremely compelling for this one body of work.

In any event, I've started you here with Cassie on the right from that vintage soap opera *Guiding Light*. It's a good thirty or forty years old and I have to tell you the truth, I've never spent much time with it until very recently. On the left we have what appears to be an extremely rabid mink. Certainly if not rabid, at least clearly stuffed.

I've spent twenty-five years going to Iceland, these are images that come out of that context and I'm going to come back to this. I'm going to come back to this work which is a piece that I'm presently developing, it's in production now, it's called *Arctic Circles*. This so-called encyclopedia is the only vanity press ency-

Pi, 1998, color iris prints (details).

clopedia ever published, actually that's not entirely true. But my vanity has been such a compelling force in the production of the work that I do not include the publishers in the process. So on the left, the first six volumes. What you see more or less is the word *Ísland*, which is the Icelandic version of Iceland. You have the colored multiplication sign in the middle, which is a volume designator, for example, pink on the lower left which is footnoted one and two for two volumes, and then my name below it. These volumes deal with the idea of identity, self-identity in relation to place. The encyclopedia is entitled *To Place* as a verb. That is, the idea of place as something becoming something, something that is evolving not only in itself but also as a product of your relation to it, the viewer's relationship to it, and the reciprocity between the view and the viewer. So one way in which this encyclopedia has been viewed is through traveling reading rooms. This particular image is a reading room in Iceland which of course was much to my delight.

The first volume: traveling over the years to Iceland I wasn't thinking of the encyclopedia. I was really thinking just about being there. And I spent a lot of time just being there. In fact I'd like to read a text about just being there. I went in 1979 on a grant, I was about twenty-four or twenty-five, and very idealistic. I was so idealistic, here I was four months, five months on this island, I hadn't spent an extensive amount of time there before—and I thought I'm not even going to bring a book. I just want to be there. You know I'll just somehow occupy myself. So there I was in my tent. This is an actual recollection called "Making Being Here Enough:"

I don't want to read, I don't want write, I don't want to do anything but be here. Doing something will take me away from being here. I want to make being here enough. Maybe it's already enough. I won't have enough to invent enough. I'll be here and I won't do anything and this place will be here but I won't do anything to it. I'll just let it be here. And maybe because I'm here and because the me in what's here makes what's here different maybe that will be enough. Maybe that will be what I'm after. But I'm not sure. I'm not sure I'll be able to perceive the difference. How will I perceive it? I need to find a way to make myself absolutely not here but still be able to be here to know the difference. I need to experience the difference between being here and not changing here and being here and changing here.

I set up camp for a night. It's a beautiful, unlikely evening after a long, rainy day. I put my tent down in an El Greco landscape. The velvet greens, the mottled purples, the rocky stubble.

But El Greco changes here, he makes being here not enough. I am here and I can't be here without El Greco. I just can't leave here alone.

And this is the paradox of my life in Iceland.

First volume, *Bluff Life*, 1982. Living on a bluff, here's your bluff, here's the lighthouse—the white dot. Two months in a fog. This photograph was a postcard. Never seen the likes of it since I've been there. One day I woke up and that bluff was an island. And it stayed an island for some time. I worked a little when I was there, I did a lot of small drawings. They were actually four-by-five inch drawings, watercolors out of this particular place. I do suspect that if I were on a different bluff or a different island this work would be different too. I don't necessarily think it would be a radical difference but it would be a sensible one, very much the way that as you move from one culture to another you see that local architecture is mostly doing the same thing, but it responds very specifically to the angle of the sun, the quantity of snow, the amount of wind, and in that dialogue creates a very different look to the architectural structure.

I thought one of the extraordinary beauties of being on this bluff would be that I would get away from the mundane. I grew up in New York more or less, and I was sick of the mundane. I found myself on an island all alone, on a bluff. I found my sense of time slowing down and synching up with the biological reality of what was present. Really to the point where I felt I could see grains of sand leveling on the beach. Entropy was screaming in my ear. So I guess the mundane really is something that's inescapable.

The second volume was titled *Folds*. *Folds* was a collection of sheep corrals. They're an indigenous form to Iceland and they are used to collect the sheep that roam throughout the mountains, or at least they were, up through the 1970s and 1980s. It is a tradition that is being curtailed because, as you know, Iceland doesn't have much vegetation, and it now has quite a bit less because of the sheep. So they have gotten rid of the sheep, more or less. And here on the left you'll see a fold in a classic style, which is an elliptical shape with the central circle. The sheep are led into the central circle, then each of the spoked areas are outlying spaces that go to different farms, and they sort the sheep this way. But what's interesting about the image is the relationship to landscape, which to me reflects an aspect of Icelandic culture I find very compelling. That is, instead of flattening the landscape or in any way compromising the geology, it will adapt to it. So in this case the fold goes up the side of the lava ridge. On the right is a very elegant, unique form in Iceland which is the herringbone pattern laying of turf, which also now, unfortunately, is no longer extant. As you can see though, one of my favorite aspects of Iceland is that everything occurs there on prime real estate. You've got 250,000 people living on an island the size of Ohio and you've got a lot of waterfront property. And I'm telling you, everything goes on on the water.

The third volume is called *Lava*. Lava is the litter of Iceland, it is the most ubiquitous presence there. I did a book which was essentially a collection of photographic drawings. The images were reproduced in the actual size of the rocks, so this is a problem with the slide thing because it's a lot of willing suspension of disbelief. These are small rocks—that little one in the left pairing, the small, perforated, figurative-looking rock which is notably my mother's favorite rock, is only about an inch and one-half high. On the left you have the pink pumice gathered over miles. You have to imagine a black ash desert and you get a little piece of pink pumice, maybe one per square mile. So these were photographic drawings, occurring specifically in the context of the book. These are not things that are presented outside of the context of this encyclopedia, which is also the context of place in Iceland.

In addition to the photographic drawings, *Lava* also included typographic drawings. On the right a double-page spread of all the names of the lava fields of Iceland. On the left, very young lava, which was collected still steaming off the ground in 1992. In these books I rarely have images of the overall landscape, but here is an image of a crater row which actually opened up in 1783, creating the largest lava flow in historic times. It changed the shape of Iceland, it changed the demographics, and it made a very pretty picture.

Fourth volume—*Pooling Waters*—a two volume set. One volume is a collection of writings and the other is a collection of photographs. These images and writings are around the theme of hot water, memory, erotica—more or less the same thing. Some of you may know that one of Iceland's key features is the dominant presence of geothermally heated water, certainly on the western coast and partially through the interior. Quite an extraordinary array of architectural forms developed around this hot water. This geothermal power plant is a prefab construction in a lava field. One of the things I love about this power plant is that behind it is one of the most popular medicinal spas in Iceland. The thing about it is you get there and it's got the look and the feel of Newark. It even has the smell. So you do have a bit of willing suspension of disbelief to imagine that this is good for you.

Swimming pools are the preferred expression of water usage. You can see the Icelandic deference to landscape in their construction. The other thing to note about Iceland is that there's very little monumentality there, partly because the economy and the population are so small. You do see it in their national sport, which is chess. This is a photograph of the oldest indoor swimming pool in Iceland from 1922. It has a fabulous story attached to it. It's in a very isolated area in the mountains on the West Fjords. It's in a tiny farm community with very few people. But when there's a community gathering they come to this building, they empty the water from the pool and they use it as a dance hall. Here is one of my favorite, almost David Lynchian swimming pools, with a picket

Tourists at Landmannalaugar, Iceland, 1992, 35mm Kodachrome.

fence which really does need to be painted white in this black ash desert. So you're driving along for a good five, ten miles and there is this little bit of steam coming up from this black ash and all of a sudden this oasis of the pool opens up to you. Its existence is kind of happenstance: the guys building the dam about fifty miles away had a little extra concrete.

One of my favorite hot pots is unfortunately tepid now. It's on a fjord, right along the edge. The tide comes in and licks the edge. It's on level with the ocean, which makes for quite a remarkable experience, and the water's carbonated so it's quite ticklish as well.

This is the beginning of the fifth volume, entitled *Verne's Journey*. Those who know Jules Verne's *Journey to the Center of the Earth* know that the entrance to the center of the earth is in Iceland. I've spent so much time there that I have no doubt of this fact. However, it is under this glacier. This is also a work which is called *Universal and False, Rorschach*. It opens the next volume and it basically puts the lie to Jules Verne's fictionalization of this extraordinary, episodic, geological wonderland in Iceland. Within a couple miles of the entrance to the center of the earth you have this incredible range of virtually architectonic geology. The center of the earth was expressed by Verne as a maelstrom, I go into the vortex here and what happens when you get into the vortex is it turns out to be ink on paper. I thought this was quite a fine metaphor for the center of the earth.

The sixth volume is called *Haraldsdóttir*, Margrét's last name being Haraldsdóttir. This was a book about the possibility of using the face to express place. I traveled with her for six months and we went to all the hot spots in Iceland. It turns out that all the hot spots are in daylight, that's an irony I enjoy. There's very little darkness there except in the winter, and there's no dark side of town. Traveling with Margrét over these six weeks, I photographed her extensively in the naturally heated outdoor pools and hot pots. I collected together quite a significant number of photographs

You are the Weather (Munich), 1997, plastic handrail insert (detail);
permanent installation at the Munich Weather Bureau, Germany.

which were eventually sequenced and formed into this book, which was very generously published by a private individual in an act of patronage which, to this day, I do not understand.

You may ask at this point what I'm doing here, talking about Iceland? So we'll get a little bit into architecture since I feel a little bit obliged. This is a recent work that was finished in 1997, it just opened in November. It is a piece called *You are the Weather, Munich*. It's located at the Meteorological Bureau in Munich, where they collect all the weather information together for use, mostly by commercial transportation. This is the entrance to the building, which is a very soft rubber material into which is inlaid a selection of adjectives. These adjectives are collected around the idea of words which apply equally to humanity and the weather. When you're on this rubber it's a bit like bedrock because it's not a veneer. It's about two inches thick and it's very soft, so it actually affects your relationship to place. In effect, it creates a larger sense of the world because it's heavier. It slows you down and it makes you more physically self-aware. On walking into the atrium you see these plastic inserts in the wood handrails—they're solid black plastic and I've inlaid chartreuse green lettering, which is in the round. So if you come at it from behind you'll see the text from behind, it's three-dimensional. These inserts punctuate eye movement throughout the atrium and eventually you move up into the instrument tower, which is six stories high. Inserted into these little hand railings you've got "foul," you've got "fine," you've got "balmy," and so on. You work your way either down to the car park or up to the instrument tower, where you encounter "nasty," "bad," and "torrid," and so on. Unfortunately I did not get a good photograph of "sultry." Finally at the top you get this incredibly non-specific word "beautiful," which seems to apply to pretty much everything and nothing.

Here is a work called *Untitled, You are the Weather*. You see, I liked this title so much that it wound up taking on many different forms and applying itself to many different works. The work is meant for a domestic space. It's an ultrasoft rubber, again with the text inlay that I just described. It's a bit like a drawing with a very composed layout, intended to keep the viewer connected to all parts of the space without hierarchy. And, as I've indicated again, my love of this text "You are the Weather" forced me to create yet another work called *You are the Weather*; that work is a four wall photo-based installation, also using this model Margrét Haraldsdóttir. In this case there's no context as far as Iceland goes, no sense of place. Here we're talking only about the viewer in relationship to the view, without hierarchy. The photographs have a very insistent, if not persistent, connection to the viewer. There are no shots of her so to speak as an object, it's all eye contact material.

I mentioned earlier that each work that I do sets no visual standard for any other work I do. Each work is in itself, although

You are the Weather, 1994/95, gelatin-silver print (detail).

conceptually there is a linear continuum. *Ellipsis* is sixty-four panels tiled together, sixty-four separate photographs. Each photograph is one foot square, so it's an eight-by-eight foot work. It's
comprised of details of the men's locker room in Reykjavík,
designed by one of my favorite Icelandic architects—there aren't
that many—Gudjón Sammúelsson. For me the locker room is
notable for its labyrinthine-like quality and the labyrinth of
voyeurism that's implied. So there are peepholes looking onto
other peepholes. The mirrors with their reflections, the tiles without any edges which effectively describe a perfect Möbius form,
and then one of my favorite details (perhaps the thing that drew
me to the space) was a collection of open and closed doors. So you
have a kind of visual and physical continuity which accentuates at
once the sensual reality of the place and the psychological expression of desire. That's *Ellipsis.*

A work called *Pooling—You*, again a photographic installation. *Pooling—You* takes off where *Verne's Journey* ended. Remember in *Verne's Journey*, you were situated at the center of the earth? What I've done here is take an infinite zoom, a blow-up in the tens of millions of percent. So basically it's an infinite zoom into the vortex, which is situated at the center of the earth. It's a four wall installation which puts the viewer at the center of the center. The photos are four-by-five foot litho images.

Briefly I'm going to go through a second group of drawings that effectively presage the photographic work. The drawings are something I've carried on over decades and they form a kind of breathing vocabulary on a daily level. These are images where you start off with two things for example, and they're cut into one. Or you start out with two forms cut into tight proximity. These are really drawings which are based in composing. When I looked up the word "to draw" in the dictionary, as I am inclined to do often with words, I found that there were twenty-two definitions, one of which was "to delineate with lines." I thought that was rather interesting. I looked at the other twenty-one definitions: all dialectic activities, to metamorphose, to translate, to take aim; basically all activities describing a dialectic interaction with a view. That's where I took off from with the idea of drawing. Now these are small drawings, they're maybe a foot square and I have to tell you that I'm giving you a very highly curtailed segment of the drawings, because they don't really interpret well in this form. These lines, for example, are not lines, they're edges. In other words, it's material and it's physical reality, they're constructions of space with a very reasonable analogy to architecture. These are the *Distant Doubles*. They are two similar drawings hung in different rooms. So it's a bit like advertising, with the image recurring in different places. Sometime in the future I hope to get into franchising.

Piece for Two Rooms. You walk in. You see a copper disc. This is from 1986, it's about seventeen inches high. You walk around it—

Things that Happen Again, 1988, two identical copper objects;
permanent installation at the Chinati Foundation, Marfa, Texas.

it's a solid copper object. It's pretty familiar but with a hint of
something less familiar. You go into the next room, the same copper disc. You walk around it, the same chronology unfolds in a different place in a different time, it's one thing. This is not a redun-
dant form, it is a cumulative one.

Piece for Two Rooms is one in a series of four different pair
objects. The pair form is an attempt to include the viewer actively
as part of the work and not just in the space between. What developed out of that was a suite of works called *Things that Happen
Again.* So you had a piece for two rooms which you've just seen, and
you have other works, *For a Here and a There* and *For a This and a That*
and *For Things That are Near.* In each one of these relationships you
have the identical pair, but each is composed in a different relation and manifesting a different identity. Here you have an object
called *Pair Field.* It's eighteen unique forms repeated. The idea was

to put together a group form that would be cohesive while allowing each individual member of that group to have its unique identity. The members are solid copper and stainless steel and none of them is larger than fifteen inches in diameter. They're dispersed in two separate rooms. The first room. James Fenimore Cooper's *The Last of the Mohicans* has a strong presence in this work. He talks about walking through the forest versus the clearing, and the way that the physical structures of the two spaces affect the syntax of your experience. So the work had a relatively sparse installation of one-half of the object and then in the other room a very crowded one, with the changing nuance in the identity of the identical objects.

And then we go back to 1980. My father owned a pawn shop in Harlem for thirty years. For a long time I've been telling people this, and I realize that they've been thinking I've been saying porn shop. I always thought that that would be good for my image. But then I didn't know what I was saying because it just occurred to me that that was what people thought. I always wondered why I was so cool. It turned out that the pawn shop is such a big part of my sense of myself, my Jewish, cultural sense. I spent a lot of time around gold. All of it was alloyed, and here I was a kid trying to reconcile Jason and the Golden Fleece to gold necklaces and things that just looked like anonymous yellow metal. So what I did was the *Gold Field*, which is kind of the inversion of Duchamp's *Dust Breeding*, which is this leveling of value. But at the same time, the gold is quite a spectacular material in itself. I used an absolutely pure gold, it is not karat gold. And it's a foil—just thick enough to hold object form. It's compression welded, there are no impurities there, it is just gold and it gives back to gold its corporeal reality and that's all it was intended to do. But what happened was I folded it and I got this incredible light coming out of it and that was the splendor of gold. Oh, *this* is Jason and the Golden Fleece (which I never understood before). I didn't like folding it. I thought it was a little bit of a didactic gesture. I let it sit as the *Gold Field*, I didn't

Asphere XI, 1986/94, solid forged steel.

show it for about ten years, I kept it in my studio wrapped up. Then in 1995 I did the pair object, *Gold Mats, Paired (for Ross and Felix)*, after my dear friend Felix Gonzalez-Torres. I understood that in pairing these two gold fields you get this ember, this fire-like glow and a perfect metaphor for intimacy and the whole use of two things as one. As opposed to the diptych, which is one thing as two.

Here is a key piece. It's called *Asphere*. It is also in a very private sense thought of as a self-portrait. It's an asphere, meaning it's not spherical and it's really not much of anything else. It is a sphere that's elongated in one dimension. So what you experience is something initially very familiar but as you spend more time with it, it becomes less and less familiar. And in that lack of fulfillment, of expectation, is my self-portrait. No, actually what happens is you kind of get the best of both worlds, it's an androgynous object, an object that includes difference as the source of its identity.

That's the *Asphere*: looks easy, experientially very complex. Most of the work looks very simple visually but experientially, which is where I focus my energy, the complexity emerges. Of course that's very much dependent on the viewer and the time they take with the view.

I've spent a lot of time thinking about and working with Emily Dickinson as I'm sure a large percentage of the audience has as well. After all she is one of the brilliant inventors of American culture across the board, and I would like to read a brief text, "When Dickinson Shut Her Eyes." It's a title that refers to a quote from Dickinson's letters, "To shut my eyes is travel," subtitled "I go to Iceland."

Recently I was reading the letters of Emily Dickinson. I began wondering about travel and Iceland too, wondering about the insistence of my returns here, about their necessity and the migratory regularity of them.

I began to wonder about travel altogether, about the how and the what of it. Travel isn't so simple as a car or a train, or as namable as a place. I thought about Emily Dickinson's travels. From the first letters she wrote she told her correspondents she didn't go out, she didn't want to go out, and that she would not come to visit them. Dickinson stayed home, insistently. Locking herself into her upstairs room, she invented another form of travel and went places.

Dickinson's invention was multiplication, herself, and empirical reach: everything that could be felt, heard, seen or smelt, everything perceptible, everything discernible from 280 Main Street, Amherst, Massachusetts. Perceptible includes the library; somehow Dickinson used the library as an empirical source, somehow she learned to consume its contents sensorially. Her library was not a source of acquired knowledge, not a tool of the intellect. Her library was simply another perceptible thing becoming another entrance, confirmation of all she sensed in the world. Even her poems about God and being dead are eyewitness.

Sequestered from the world, knowing that going out into it hampered her ability to invent it, Dickinson stayed home except for two summer trips to Cambridge as a child and one to Washington later in life. Dickinson stayed home when Ralph Waldo Emerson visited her brother next door. Her business was circumference.

In her verse Dickinson spoke of Vesuvius at home. In her letters she said she traveled when she closed her eyes, and that she went to sleep as though it were a country. In her room alone, she said, was freedom. Here she wrote one thousand seven hundred and seventy-five poems. Dickinson shut her eyes and went places this world never was.

For the time being, Dickinson's here with me—in Iceland. For someone who stayed home she fits naturally into this distant and necessary place. Her writing is an equivalent of this unique island; Dickinson invented a syntax out of herself, and Iceland did too—volcanoes do. Dickinson stayed home to get at the world. But home is an island like this one. And I come to this island to get at the very center of the world.

This is something of the manner in which Dickinson has catalyzed my relationship to myself, and what I'm doing so regularly in Iceland. *How Dickinson Stayed Home* is a piece that quotes from her letters: "My business is circumference." They are blocks of aluminum and plastic, both solid. The bigger the space, the more circuitous the pun.

One of the only bodies of work that I actually conceived of as existing effectively in domestic space—or should I say with the intention of existing in domestic space, *The Key and Cues. The Key and*

Cues are a collection of first lines of Emily Dickinson: "What we see we know somewhat," "Crisis is a hair," "To make a prairie it takes a clover and one bee," "The zeroes taught us phosphorus," "An hour is a sea"—some of the first lines.

I'm going to cut back very briefly to an earlier work. I'm trying to get this thing to be a little bit more about architecture. In 1982-1983 I did a work called *Cobbled Leads*. This was, much to my delight, in an Otto Klenze building, the Glyptotek in Munich. This type of architecture speaks largely in symbolic terms, for example the door to the inner courtyard is something like forty feet high. So the first thing you know is you're struggling to get into the space. And that scale is not so much about human presence as it is about polemical and ideological issues. I decided to insert this rather quiet, virtually invisible triangle, which is a collection of lead cobblestones cast after the Czechoslovakian granite stones they replace. It is basically twenty-two tons of lead in the ground. Now the reason I bring up that statistic—which is not terribly interesting in itself—is to give you a sense of the physical presence of what was in the ground. It was virtually invisible but it created a kind of leverage, breaking the symmetry of the space. So as you traversed the edge of the triangle, you felt this pull to the left, which was all of this weight pulling the perfection in symmetry and scale of the overall courtyard. It was just simply tearing it very quietly. Also lead is a very soft material, very quiet. So you walked from the granite and the travertine, and you hit the lead and you were on a larger world and you were in a quieter place and that's what the work was. The irony is that while it was supposed to be a permanent work it was ripped out. So then it seemed to me that the piece became Sisyphean—taking twenty-two tons of lead stones from the ground. Here was a work that didn't take up any space and mostly nobody could even see, and it was ripped out.

And then we move into a recent work which takes us back to Basel, a piece called *Yous in You*. The architectural firm of Zwimpfer

Cobbled Leads, 1983, lead cobblestones; Glyptotek, Munich, Germany (destroyed).

Yous in You, 1997, study for a permanent installation at
Bahnhof Ost Basel, Switzerland.

and Partners are developing the site along the East train station in
Basel, it's a collection of six buildings and five interceding niches.
Along this rather vast array of buildings, which is at least six hundred feet long, there is a walkway which is where I've been asked to
get involved. I should also mention that early on in the design
phase of this rather large building, Don Judd was involved in the
design of the façade.

In any event, my involvement with this work was in part an
homage to Don Judd. My proposal was to insert a path, which is the
idea of a place that is very much a part of the place, but it sets you
in a questioning relationship to that place. I decided to pave the
walkway with two-inch thick rubber, colored a classic earthen
orange, associated with early rubber production. At the entrances
to the different buildings there will be concrete mats which are
cast from the same molds. These molds come from a place in Ice-

land. It's a unique geologic form, where the basalt columns form a plane. I thought to quote this original, organic tiling pattern in a place with a very highly developed, platonic symmetry, which is the way these buildings will express themselves to the viewer as they move through them. The idea of the path here is to create a very complex surface visually, without affect. What will happen is you're going to have these hexagonally cut tiles with this hexagonal impression taken from Iceland, and you're going to have areas of hard and soft rubber without any visual confirmation of the change in this tactile experience. So as you move along, the desire is that this experience will become more self-reflexive, more complex and it will give you an edge or a view into what it isn't, which are the buildings around it. There are also niches which have benches covered with soft rubber. The balustrade is also covered with this very sensuous, very soft, almost S&M rubber. You have your concrete and your rubber tiles, and the rubber again is very thick so there's a very strong sense of place that comes out of that weight. So it's quite complex and three-dimensional. The benches are a little bit overstated. Some niches have a crowded bench arrangement for more social activity and other niches will have single benches for a solitary experience. In all cases the benches will be located in a manner that will not allow you to confirm the platonic aspect of the view. In other words, they will all be skewed and they will never be quite right.

Now I'm going to bring you back to the beginning to close this circle off fairly quickly. On the left we have Dinah, also from *Guiding Light*, and on the right we have this recurring rabid mink. These again are images taken out of Iceland, all of the photography comes out of Iceland for the most part. The issue with the mink is particularly spectacular in Iceland because they brought this animal in—can you imagine bringing something into your country that looked like that? I mean it's one thing if it was already there, but you bring it in? So that's one thing. So they brought it in, it got loose and it devastated a number of different ecological cycles in Iceland. I've been spending the last few years up on the northern tips of Iceland, where it intersects the Arctic Circle. I've collected together a group of images which are based conceptually around circular and cyclical events. The work was originally titled *Arctic Circles*, but now I call it *Pi*. It occurs on four walls, it's forty-five photographs and it's set up in a way that the architectural setting has a lot to do with how you read the piece.

You may be wondering how *Guiding Light* could possibly be inserted into such an apparently intelligent context. The fact is that *Guiding Light* is one of the dominant activities in rural Iceland today. In Northern Iceland it was definitely the five to six o'clock, no competition situation.

I grew up with the Arctic Circle on the map and there was no question in my mind that I was going to go look at it one day, and I did so. Of course it is a dead ringer for any other horizon, but it is the Arctic Circle. I collected together images of the Circle, cropped them vertically and then dispersed these images along the four walls of the room among the other images. It sews together the themes and gives continuity to these disparate images. You have to imagine all of these images collected together and repeated in various fashions. There are images of a kind of smirking Arctic fox, and of people I came to know in the process of doing the piece, including Björn and Hilde, who make their living in this area harvesting eider down feathers. Other images in the piece include a single egg eider nest, which is a very rare occurrence, shots of a snowy owl on a piece of lava, and fields of dead birds. And the last and closing shot of this lecture which is also a work by itself, called *Dead Owl*. The most recent pair form.

Robert Irwin

The last speaker (Roni Horn) took the wind out of my sails. I'm sort of a little overwhelmed; I really enjoyed it. The thing I like about being an artist among artists is that none of us defines art, we do it collectively. It's really a treat every now and then to see someone do something that you know nothing about. Who takes you down paths and into places that you would never think to go, and does it with authority. It was really a treat. In many ways I would rather just sort of sit right now and think about it; it was an incredible experience. Plus she's a spectacular speaker I must say.

Given that idea that we collectively make art, let me press the point and talk about a world where when you look up and see a white puff in the sky, you don't first think that it's a cloud or tell me it's a cumulous cloud or predict rain, nor do you try to tell me it looks just like a white bunny rabbit, and thus miss the unique moment of pure perception. A world in which, while everything has the potential to be a sign, symbol, or metaphor for something else, it also has its pure presence, just what it is. I think that world, what I will call the world of the phenomenal, is the essential issue within the history of modern art. The fundamental idea that this pure perception is the pure subject of art. And that as a pure subject, this art has no actual physical properties. This art resides in the pure void of discovery. Whatever it is, we collectively define it with our actions. And while each generation of artists makes an art, which may be a perfect representation of their unique moment in time and is art, none of these arts is art per se.

Our problem is we have all been educated to a wonderful series of objects as art. This, coupled with the prevailing aspiration of classical thought, a timeless art, and it is no wonder that we mistakenly mix up the object as the subject. Let me suggest that while there is no transcendental art, there is an infinite subject that every generation of artists has to address if they are going to make any sense out of their own time.

On the grounds of that statement, I'd like to make my own short history to understand the idea of my making a garden as a work of art.

Here I would like to begin with a quote by Piet Mondrian:

Non-figurative art brings to an end the ancient culture of art. The culture of particular form is approaching its end, the culture of determined relations has begun.

I think that's quite a prediction and I'm going to act on that a little bit. Several times in the previous talks the term "public art," and the idea of public art as interfacing with sculpture, has been brought up. I think one of the myths of our time is that the term "public art" and the term "art in public places" mean the same thing. I would like to put up for consideration that there is, at this moment, a history of art that brings me to the imperative to act out my art inquiry in the public realm, to question the validity and the intent of modern thought in public practice. That's a hell of a responsibility. If it means for the moment crossing over some boundaries and stepping on some toes, I'm afraid I'm going to have to do that. I have to say at the same time that you're going to have to be kind to me because I've never had more contradictions, more difficulties, and more questions in my life. So while I like the thrust of my questions, I am at the same time riddled with doubt. This is not to be taken as a weakness.

The critical history of modern art, as I understand it, is approximately two hundred years old. It begins at the end of the eighteenth century with a beautiful painting, put together with an incredible pictorial reality: David's *Coronation of Napoleon*. And within a hundred years, we are asked to confront a simple white square on a white ground and to take it seriously. To me that is a radical history and it is in this sense that changes cause revolutions, much more than revolutions cause change. I think the philosopher Edmund Husserl best framed the critical issue at work here when he spoke of the need for a "phenomenological reduction." A stripping away, Husserl advised, a bracketing out of the cocoon of our pervasive knowledge, to return, for the moment, to our perceptual roots in the world, where we can ask the fundamental question: How could it be otherwise?

There have only been a few such radical movements in our histories. The Copernican revolution comes to mind, and St. Thomas Aquinas's use of Aristotle to set in motion the Enlightenment. Most of our histories are homogeneous in character. That is, our most basic concepts and beliefs remain in place, as ground upon which we orderly build those most intricate structures that underwrite all of our disciplines and social practices.

The very idea of going back to our beginnings as phenomenal beings in the world and putting up for examination our most cherished beliefs, besides being radical, is very frightening. So when at the end of the nineteenth century, having arrived at Malevich's white on white, when even his friends declared that "all is lost, that everything we recognize, know and believe is gone, you have left us with nothing but an empty desert," Malevich declared, "Ah yes, but it is a desert of pure feelings." In effect, with this declaration, Malevich put in place the philosophic ground of modern art. Setting in motion modern art's direct confrontation with philosophy's most basic question: whether or not individual human beings do, in fact, choose and set in motion their own meaning. This focus on the individual has often been misappropriated and trivialized by linking it to the term "expression"—that what artists are doing is expressing themselves. But the fact is, everything we do is a form of expression in one way or another, so that popular myth is a red herring.

In his turn, Piet Mondrian laid out for us in a clear, systematic exposition in his work the conceptual grounds for modern art. I remember as a young artist thirty years ago seeing a large retrospective of his work in New York. It began with a beautifully rendered drawing of a tree, followed by a series of paintings revealing the other levels of the tree's being, exposing its underlying structure, its physicality, and finally, its energies, culminating in the plus-minus paintings. All misinterpreted as some kind of abstraction. But let me state here that no artist worth their salt has ever made an abstract art; every artist makes their art as real as is possible. What is at stake here is what we mean by the term real.

Having now accomplished the phenomenological reduction and established both the philosophic and conceptual grounds of modern art, it was left to the abstract expressionists, from Pollock to Newman, Reinhardt to DeKooning, to supply us with a new visual vocabulary and the syntax for it. I should note, in my haste, I have left out an important caveat in Husserl's reduction, what he called "bracketing out." The idea is that this phenomenological reduction is not an either/or proposition, but instead a setting aside for the moment of the old pictorial logic. This important idea underwrites a critical element in modern thought, that two truths can, and do, exist simultaneously. This is a basic tenet of modern thought that directly challenges the old hierarchical structuring of classical thought, where truth either is, or it isn't.

Having flashed through one hundred and fifty years of art history, we now come to the point where, as second generation

Abstract Expressionists, my generation was left with an incredible legacy of questions. The mark was no longer tied directly to a system of signs; scale, color, etc. were free agents having a life of their own. The loss of the sign-human figure required a new, more critical humanism. The mark no longer led inevitably to a positive/negative meaning structure, and a frame to painting was no longer sacrosanct.

The number of red herrings abounded: that the breaking of the frame could be resolved in sculpture, that non-objective would translate to be non-object, that Marxist critics actually knew something, or worse, Greenberg's warning that this history of modern art was never intended to go so far. That flatness was an issue in the late twentieth century. But here Mondrian's words again give us guidance: "The culture of determined relations has begun." Ideas of order are not limited to things and objects held in the vacuum of abstract meaning structures, instead they can now be referenced and understood in the continuum of their immediate contextual ground.

Thinking about that, and trying to make some kind of sense out of all that as an artist—I have, at one point, been a painter, but lost painting as a way of thinking—I briefly became a sculptor and found even more questions. I lost my studio, worked with pure light and space and threatened to disappear altogether. But the questions were too rich to stop and seemed too essential to give up on. Besides, when I looked around, there were no frames in my perception, instead the world around me knitted together into a continuous envelope.

The idea of abandoning painting and moving out of the studio was bewildering to me. I liked being a painter and I liked being in the studio. It certainly raised a lot of questions, not the least of which was: What do I do now? How do I recognize and make sense of an art that suddenly intersects directly with all of nature? The problem is that all information is contextually bound and all understanding is understanding within a frame of reference. So when we think to break such a time-honored reference like the frame to painting, after the initial euphoria of simply breaking out, you find you've lost something of critical value, which is the common agreement that binds our entire collective understanding together. Think about it for just a second. If I make a mark within the frame of the painting, to anyone conversant with the whole history of painting, that mark can be weighed with and against the whole history of marks, allowing for the most sophisticated kind of dialogue, while for the moment I've gained only the crude in and out. Making the critical question for art in public places: What would be the extended frame of reference for the practice of art outside the traditional forum? And how are we to make all of those critical identifications and judgements so necessary to everyday practice?

Our first clue comes in the most obvious of places—the conflicting use of two terms seemingly interchangeable but actually meaning something quite different. One, the term "public art," which indicates some kind of immediate social interface or social service, and two, the term "art in public places," which indicates to me a continuation of the inquiry that is the arrow of modern art history that I have sketched out for you. Phenomenological reduction, philosophic ground, conceptual ground, a new visual vocabulary, and now the inquiry as to how we might practice from a modern aesthetic.

Understand that as an artist propelled by the trajectory of this history of modernism, I find now the talk of postmodernism, deconstructivism, and public art slightly hilarious. How can you talk about most anything when it will be at least two hundred more years before we find out the full consequences of modernism? If that isn't a red herring, I'll kiss your ass.

As I see it, the advent of an "art in public places" at a precise moment is an historical imperative. Already having had our philosophic, our conceptual grounds, and a new language, having these things all in place—now comes the time when we begin to try to find out how it works. To actually practice it. So I lost the luxury of a studio, where the beauty is that I can make the world look anyway I want as long as I don't expect anyone else to agree with me; but the minute I put myself in a public realm, especially with the ambition I had, I enter an ethical no man's land. I'm suddenly coming to all these projects with an interest, a curiosity, and a pursuit that is not necessarily one for which they've asked me to come. So I made a couple of very simple adjustments in my life, simple in that they've also been rather clumsy. First, I can't just go around proposing things for other people's backyards, since in this guise I'm a carpetbagger. Second, I can't proselytize, stand on corners like a Christian telling everybody within earshot they need the "truth" of my art. Third, I can't solicit anything from anybody, since the world doesn't give me a living for indulging myself. The one thing I can do is answer the telephone. The Getty was just such a call. As it turned out it was an incredible opportunity to do almost a case study to find out whether or not all of my bullshit really held water or not.

I'll just move on to the slides and talk a bit about how the Getty project developed. The general way I respond to such invitations is to say I will come and look, no strings attached—it's what I do best. Initially, I just spend time wandering around the site and the area with no ambitions for it. Just scratching my ass, running my hands over it, developing a kind of intimacy for it. It's the one thing that artists bring to a project that architects just talk about, they don't have the time for it. I mean intimacy in the sense that Don Judd had with Marfa, or the kind of hands-on involvement that Roni Horn just exhibited for Iceland.

After a while sometimes I have a good feeling about a place, and if I can think of something worth the doing, something that makes sense for all my reasons, I make a proposal. And then they,

Central Garden for the Getty Center, Los Angeles, California; 1997. Aerial view
of the Getty site; the garden is the area of the hole in the foreground.

for all their rhymes and reasons, can decide whether it makes good
sense for them. Then and only then, we can talk about how to get
it done. I should add there is another element in the process that
is as much a part of the work as the built project itself. I very much
insist that they take individual responsibility for the development
of the work. After all, it is in their backyard. They're the ones who
have to live with it, and, I hope, get real pleasure out of it. Unfortunately, a lot of projects fall apart because we're not able to
bridge that gap. Ideas are only as good as the change they make in
our lives. To put ideas in the world and honor them simply as
objects or art, and not let them change our lives, is not to honor
them at all.

I almost never show slides and the main reason is I hate to hold
the quality of the dialogue and the quality of the ideas to my success or failure. I'm just taking a swing at it like everybody else.

I was asked to come to the Getty because there was some discomfort with the project becoming too much of one piece. They really wanted somebody to intervene and create some kind of a counterpoint, which by definition was to ask me to go to war with Richard Meier. It was very naive on their part, but the Getty wants to think of itself as a populist activity, and surprisingly enough they are to a great degree. They wanted us to collaborate so bad they could taste it. It wasn't possible. Richard wanted to do it and I understood his concern, he essentially saw it as his project and he saw me as somebody painting on his canvas. I had empathy for his discomfort, which he still has. It turned out to be for me a very interesting interrelationship—for one year, we essentially competed. Once a month we met with the Getty people, once a month he came with a plan as to how it should be, and I came with a plan as to how it might be. It was a good exercise for me, because it was a chance to find out how my thinking faired in that kind of an environment. It was always held in his office and he always brought along someone whose job it was to shoot down my proposal logistically. Someone else would be there to shoot it down economically, and then he also had an intellectual apologist at each meeting. I take some pride in that over the years I chewed up three intellectual apologists.

It was interesting, you'd never define collaboration in those terms. Nevertheless, it turned out to be very successful. As I worked through the year with his ninety-man office pitted against me— David and Goliath as they say—the project continually improved. Strangely enough, it just kept getting better. Somehow, I managed to turn the challenge and hostility into a positive. And, as I told the Getty people, "I'll play this game as long as it keeps getting better," and it did keep getting better. Eventually, even they realized that there was no way that I could pass all the material through Meier's office, and so I was allowed to essentially create a second contract and put together my own group of people to work with. It was important for me to have my own people since I was on a major

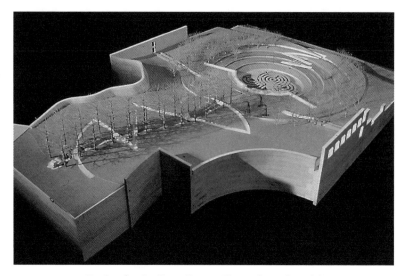

Garden for the Getty Center. Clay and wood model
of the "bones" of the garden.

learning curve. I still am on a major learning curve—each project
being different, I find myself constantly over my head. I'm always
learning, and when people say to me, "Are you sure you can do
this?" the answer is always, "No, I'm not sure." This was especially
the case in the very beginning when we would have these con-
frontations and they would say, "Well this seems to be a problem,
what do you think Richard?" And Richard would say, "Well, by
damn, here's the answer." And he'd give them the answer every
time, which was startling to me because I would have to say, "Shit,
I'm gonna have to go home and think about that." So we went
through this exercise for a long while and in the very beginning I
did not really have any idea where the project was going to go or
what the nature of it was going to be. Given the scale of the project, there were moments that raised a lot of funny questions for
me. The idea of working conditionally did work out in the end.

Garden for the Getty Center.
Construction of azalea rings.

The space of the garden is almost on a living room scale, hence the conditions of this space are clearly architectonic. My first concern was that, while there was an interest on the part of the Getty that the garden be an important counterpoint in the experience of the Getty, the space had come into being without its having generated any of the decisions of its becoming. The space was simply left over, which, by definition, is a clear contradiction in terms. Interestingly, this anomaly was, as it turned out, a rich opportunity; since nobody in their right mind would ever design such a space, when I turned it around and made its strange eccentricity and asymmetry work for me, it became instantly unique, something you're not likely to come upon again.

The second challenge was to establish a scale for the garden that would hold its own with the impressive scale of the architecture. In conjunction with this issue of scale, the garden space was too small to carry out all the desires the Getty had for its use, requiring that early on I develop a scheme to capture what had been a down slope and turn it around into what is now the lower third of the garden.

The fourth and most challenging issue was to conceive how to create the crossover from the hard geometry and scale of the architecture to the more intimate and delicate nature of the plant material. In the end, I wanted you to become immersed in the garden and capable of focusing on the beauty of one flower. So the entire garden is a slow descent into a contemplative place.

The first gesture was to put the upper level of the garden back into its more natural canyon form. I would like to have it steeper, but there is a binding issue in the world: how do you provide access for the disabled? This problem turned out to be a positive. While the initial plan did the obvious, the path following the stream down, it made the descent too short and too shallow. When I gave up on the idea to simply accommodate the disabled, and rather let that need drive the plan, the result was the eccentric zig-zag pattern you see in the slide. A far more interesting feel of traversing back and forth each time, passing in and out of the stream area, gives you a chance to actually engage the space and the architecture. A more mesmerizing descent where every crossing is accented by a different set of water sounds, a different rock and water pattern, and where at each crossing the plant and material varies in color, pattern, texture, even smell. Just as importantly, the strength of the configuration and added weight of the extended overlapping of experience give the garden the kind of power to hold its own in the context.

This is an overlay of the planting plan. This is an overlay of the tree forms, which are very critical to this plan. This is just an image, because my trees aren't fully grown. I should say that because of the strong geometry of the building, everything in the garden, especially on the outside, begins with geometry. Maybe in

Garden for the Getty Center. Zig-zag path,
early first winter planting.

this sense, I actually was a friend of Richard's. In almost every case
this is compounded so that the first time you experience it, you
experience it as pattern. Moreover, in many cases it's compounded
so that the first level of experience is as texture. As Roni said, a key
element has to do with the changes of surface, the tactile quality
of the surface, the differences of the inclines, the rate of descent.
All of these kinds of things were critical to how it worked. Ultimately, I think the trees will be one of the major elements in what
is now a very young garden. In California there are not very many
trees that have the stature that trees have in the east, but I finally
found a tree that seemed best. It's called a London Plane, it's a very
formal sycamore tree, and you see them in the Luxembourg Gardens as a large hedge. You have to buy a tree that's no older than
two years old, because in the industry now they corrupt all trees by
the end of the second year. They either top them off to force them

to bush out or to grow faster, so if you want a good, single leader that you can grow on to be a great tree, you have to buy it and wait ten years for it grow. One of the main reasons why the Getty project was such a great opportunity was their willingness to take care and maintain the garden. Most of the projects I am asked to do, they want me to know how important it's going to be: "It's going to be the entrance to the west, the symbol of all mankind, the history of the last two hundred years." And you say to them, "What's your maintenance?" and they say, "Huh?"

The idea that you can plan something without having thought about whether or not you're willing or able to maintain it, is the reason why all the plazas in this country are turning into hardscape. They've become hostile places in my mind. It's become very difficult to find a real nice place to actually sit in the city anymore. Add to this the fact that nobody's willing to wait for a tree to grow. These are not questions of economics, as they would have you think; they're issues of values, and values are an integral part of the whole process of what I think being an artist is. Anyway, the idea is that ultimately this stand of trees will go down the slope with a very open, kind of feathery geometry to it, totally organic in the center and grown together. It's something I'm dying to see and I've only got seven more years to wait.

This is the construction site about two and one-half months before the opening. Literally. I don't think Meier did it on purpose but he kept making changes and they couldn't take this crane out of there until literally one month before the thing opened, which made the whole thing an interesting adventure.

Let me go back to the problem of the trees to make a point. It's an interesting thing you have to do, that is, to know you don't know, and to be willing to put yourself on a long learning curve. You have to spend a lot of time doing a variety of research. Looking for the right tree I started out with some of Meier's advisors, a couple of very major landscape architects, and they recommended

Garden for the Getty Center. Construction site,
looking down the slope.

that I should use a cultivar of the London Plane, called a bloodgood. I asked everybody and there was a common agreement that
the bloodgood was the right tree. So I went to Oregon and handpicked all of my bloodgood trees, gave them all a kiss and went
back to write the check to buy them, and I ran into a funny guy
named Barry Coat. Barry Coat just said to me, "Uh, you don't want
a bloodgood, what you want is a yarwood." And I said, "Yeah,
c'mon what do you mean a yarwood?" And he said, "You want a
yarwood." I went back and asked all these people again, all ten of
them: "A yarwood?" And they said, "No, no, no, a bloodgood, you
know here's a yarwood, they're all performing badly." So I went
back to Barry Coat, I liked his demeanor. Every time you'd walk
through a parking lot with him, you'd look over and he'd be way
over at the edge hugging a tree, talking about its problems and its
difficulties. This man is incredible when it comes to trees. It's also

Garden for the Getty Center. The Arbor Plaza,
end of zig-zag path.

a part of the story of my incompetence level in this thing. In talking to Barry, I went back and asked, "Why the yarwood?" He said, "Well you know, the yarwood was introduced only about eight years ago and because of the industry being in a hurry, they took the yarwood and budded them onto a bloodgood stock. All of the yarwoods everybody is seeing are not real yarwoods. They're essentially bastardized, and in fact, in the industry some of these people are going to get sued." I decided I liked what Barry Coat had to say, so I rushed back. I had walked by some beautiful yarwoods and I found the last yarwoods in existence and brought them down to California. And Richard Meier's landscape people all brought their bloodgoods down. In the first year out in the valley when we came to spring, I'm happy to report mine were all green and his were all brown. Moreover, it answered one of their questions: "What do you know about doing landscape?" The answer is not much, but you

Garden for the Getty Center. Plaza bridge over stream at Carnelian granite wall. Chadder waterfall, curved steps.

know you have to do enough homework because you don't do projects like this on your own; you have to find the Barry Coats of the world to work with. That's my tree story.

Once I had the tree I came to realize that both of my stands of trees, the London Plane and the Crepe Myrtes in the lower bowl, are deciduous. Add the large border of Mullenbergia Risen grass along both sides of the stream that needed to be cut back in the winter, and I found myself with an unexpected opportunity to have a winter season in the garden, something unusual for California.

This is a planting plan, the initial one for the whole garden. I've had my own planting ground in San Diego, and we've been working with the plant material for about three and one-half years now. I've found a young gardener, Jim Duggan, who was laying tile to survive. He runs a little nursery, more a garden of his own, and we now spend a lot of time in nurseries, a lot of time talking plants and hugging each other—it's a very funny world, the plant world. They're a very lovable group of people.

This is the beginning of the path as you start on down. In the first sort of swing around you can see the stone that's been laid in. I didn't have enough money to lay the stone all the way around, which turned out to be a plus. The stone—all the material in the garden by the way—is material that will wear or season well. The walls here are Cor-ten steel and the decks are teak. Each time you start out, it's essentially out on the grass. You'll pass through these tall areas of grass once they're grown and enter the stream area where the wood bridges are. At that point, you cross over the stream and each time you cross it has a different physical quality. The stone is laid differently and it has a different sound. I've tuned the sound so that each time you cross over the bridge the sound is actually different on the left and right. And each time you pass through, the character and the quality of the plant material is different. I hope it's subtle enough so that you're not conscious of the details in themselves, but at the end of it you say, "Wow, that was really nice." Maybe you'll have to come back four more times to find out why the wow was there.

In thinking about the plant material, I talked to many different plant people for a long time. I went to nurseries not only in California, but also in Oregon, Arizona, Texas, and up into Washington, because of the limited palette in the industry. Essentially everybody raises what people buy and people buy what everybody raises. It's a kind of Catch-22. Therefore, if you want to extend the vocabulary you really beat the bushes, you have to find the individual plant lovers. I eventually had a spectacular palette, it's so rich you can drown in this palette. The levels, dimensions, the quality of color, and the richness of texture are beyond anything I've ever dealt with before. It is spectacular. Again this has to do with doing a tremendous amount of homework—every single plant in the garden is handpicked. There are over three hundred species;

Garden for the Getty Center. Ring paths in lower bowl arcs.

Garden for the Getty Center. View of lower bowl,
first year summer planting.

most gardens have maybe twenty or thirty. To hold this all together
we have a few strategies going. One, which was extremely successful, was to take common plants and make them a kind of backbone
for the garden; they're very good and successful plants. The
bougainvillea in California is an example. It blooms nine months
of the year and its bloom is a spectacular display—the only problem is that people have habituated to it and it's become somewhat
ordinary. Referring to Mondrian's quote about context, the plants
are never thought of as single elements or as specimen plants;
everything is constantly interwoven with everything else. We tried
to take these familiar plants and put them in unfamiliar relationships, to reintroduce them, to reinvigorate them.

In the beginning I had trouble communicating with the landscape people. I'd tell them what I wanted things to feel like, they'd
rattle off some Latin terms, and I'd say, "Yeah. Well, maybe." They'd

say, "Well, it's going to look pink and green." And I'd say, "Really?" I'd look at a little plant and I'd say it looks terrific and they'd say, "Nah, it ain't going to look like that, it's going to be this big and that large." We had a very hard time in the beginning that led me to doing large collages. I bought a couple of thousand dollars worth of plant books and cut them up unmercifully. These huge collages became the media of our dialogue, and they were fun and educational for both of us.

The plant material in the stream area is first thought of in terms of its leaf color, the flowers are thought of as a bonus. So the plant material as such is orchestrated in terms of the greens and then there's always a kicker color—the green that activates the whole thing. The first time you walk through at the top area the plants are low; I want you to be able to see out from underneath the trees. The second time you pass through, you look out through a window form. The third time you pass through, you're totally enclosed. So with each pass the height of the plant changes the character of it, and the level of texture, and the level of color, and the nature of the color changes.

This is one of the bench areas, note the use of steel. The use of the Cor-ten was a key element. Cor-ten steel is something which was developed for architecture, I've seen it in a couple of situations where I thought it was interesting. It fell out of fashion some time ago, but in a garden it's actually a very interesting material. First, I needed to get the disabled down, so I couldn't let the path ride up on the surface. The path is laid out literally to within an eighth of an inch to maximize the fall. I wanted the path to cut into the slope and then out again. The Cor-ten was a way of creating that cut so that it appeared as if the earth has been cut away. And rather than having to build little stone walls or concrete walls which would have become clumsy, the Cor-ten gives you the clean geometry that is critical in this context. If it's sandblasted and then very carefully watered for a couple of months it gets a surface which is very tactile, almost like velvet. Ultimately it will be a very dark, rich, violet brown.

One of the things about details like the benches and the railings is that I was tempted to design them within an inch of their lives, because I don't get very many opportunities to do that sort of thing. As the project developed, I felt that all of those things had to be very understated so that they became more a part of the whole. I didn't want them to stand out as items in and of themselves. I let everything happen in the craft. The bench is a very straightforward bench, yet every piece of wood is shaped on all four sides and carefully fitted. Believe it or not, it's actually comfortable; it's a nice place to sit.

I started out wanting the trees to be able to grow together, meaning they couldn't really be more than twenty-two or twenty-three feet apart. That forced the stream to be confined into a rather narrow area, and at first I thought that I was going to make a natural stream of some kind. When it became confined because of the geometry, I started thinking about it in a formal sense, which was totally wrong for what I was doing. What I actually did was turn the stream into a piece of sculpture. By the way, I should say that this is not a garden in the true sense of the word; this is a sculpture in the form of a garden that aspires to be art. It's a slightly different approach to the whole thing.

I started looking for stone, which was a great adventure. I went up in Montana, up in the gold country of California, in Idaho, and out to West Virginia and Pennsylvania. The stone on the walk is from West Virginia and Pennsylvania. I found a stone that I really liked in that it fractured geometrically, so it wasn't a boulder that tumbled down the stream and was rounded off; it was a rock that fractured in these really interesting ways. I handpicked each one of the stones, I brought them down and then had the great fun of having two 120-ton cranes standing there and saying, "Move it just a little to the left there." In the beginning, it looked chaotic and

Garden for the Getty Center. View of garden at early completion (winter).

scared the hell out of everybody. But this is where things began to change. In the beginning, the people working on the job weren't exactly hostile, but they were certainly not sympathetic or friendly. For example, I told the welders how I wanted the steel welded; I talked about chamfering the edges, and I asked that two welders operate simultaneously on both sides to prevent warping the steel. They all looked at me and said, "Yeah, okay, you know." They'd only been welding for thirty years, what did this guy know. So they went out and warped the first couple of plates and then we sat down, talked about it, and then they went back and did these incredibly beautiful weld jobs. It was a marvelous level of craft; in the end they all brought their families to show them what they'd done, and it was an interesting celebration of their skills, nobody ever asks them to really do what they do, because they're so estranged from their craft by the economics and expediency. But once they got into it, they loved doing what they were really good at.

Going back to making my stream. This is the beginning of building the stream and it doesn't look like a stream at all, it was kind of scary trying to figure how things were going to work at this stage. It's difficult to set boulders and to project how high they're going to be and what they're going to look like, let alone how the water and sound were going to work. I wanted a stone that really had strength to clad the sides. I found this material up near Kalispol, Montana. Then we began setting the stones, which as I said, was really a fun thing to do. The first time you cross you don't see the water at all, the stone sits right up next to the bridge. I made these cavities between the rock as speakers and I configured the bottom of the stream so that the sound of the water is changed and broadcast up through the cavities. The first time you walk through you hear the sound but you don't see the water. The second time, the water dams up and spills over some smaller rocks, and becomes quite playful. In the third area it begins to course between the rocks with a gurgling sound, and then as it gets down to the bottom it goes through a different configuration. There's a transition area where the stream now spreads out to course over the flat plaza. It was very important that the stream have a real strong visual pattern to it, and yet it had to be absolutely shallow. If not, I'd have had to put a fence around it, declare it a swimming pool, and hire a lifeguard. It's interesting how necessity begins to drive the creative process to ideas that would never otherwise arise. The stream becomes stepped and the water breaks over a series of points that are laid up into the stream. The whole bottom of the stream is laid with stone on edge. This creates a criss-cross patterning of the water, and the running water makes a very low, very sensual sound as it passes over this rough surface. From the top to the bottom, the stream changes five times in sound and physical characteristics. I found a mountain of shale up in Montana where these small chips of rock had been breaking off for centuries. I brought it down and we laid it in these criss-crossing patterns, which I really rather like. Then it goes over the edge of a large Carnelian granite wall and drops twenty feet into a pool area below.

The plaza works as both a meeting place/refuge and a transition/connecting element between the zig-zag of the upper garden and the radiating oval configuration of the lower garden. The element on the plaza with the greatest responsibility for knitting everything together are the two sets of umbrella-shaped arbors made out of rebar, which is among the cheapest materials made. And even though the form has a kind of unity to it, I really think you see these forms first as a kind of textural experience—the idea of something which is repeated so often that it becomes understood as much by its parts as its whole—with these forty-four one inch bars going up and intersecting with forty-four three-quarter inch bars fanning out at the top. Eventually bougainvillea will grow up inside of them and they'll become a bower of flowers. The bougainvillea is now just starting to grow; it got the hell kicked out of it in the early going.

I didn't have the money to build the wall as I wanted. It's a Carnelian granite from South Dakota, but it's unlike Meier's stones on the buildings, which are cut and laid very intricately. I had to use a brick technology, so to make it interesting I started the wall straight up and down on the ends, and then slowly tilted it back, first to five percent at the corner, then to seven percent, and finally twenty-three percent at the center. The wall's increasingly articulated all the way around where the water cascades down the center.

One of the things I should mention is that I reserved color. Since Richard Meier was not allowed to use color—which of course he wouldn't have used anyway—I reserved color as my kicker. As you go down in the garden, the further and further you go the more and more colorful it gets. I like to say that the flower garden is going to become exuberant by the end.

One other thing I didn't mention is that the garden faces south so that all of the feature plants as you descend are intended to be back lit, and when you return up the path, the feature plants are those that are best seen front lit. The whole garden is thought through in that way.

The entire bottom of the pool was laid in stone, piece by piece in a circular pattern. It was one of those seeming excesses that the garden really needed. The process of coming to that conclusion reflects my slow learning curve—they'd say, "What do you think the bottom of the pool should be?" I realized I'd never thought about what the bottom of the pool should be. So I started looking at the bottom of pools elsewhere, and it turns out that the bottom of pools are the worst; they're usually discolored, peeling or they've got algae covering them. There's no technology that makes the bottom of a pool nice and here I was, looking straight down on it, from twenty feet above into eighteen inches of water. It became

Garden for the Getty Center.
One of the garden's inhabitants.

a really critical item. It was a very hard sell to convince them that I absolutely had to lay all this stone, but in the end it was the right solution.

Everyone tells me the azaleas are not going to succeed. But that's one of the fun things about being an artist, I can be impractical and roll the dice. I've been rolling the dice most of my life and I've failed many times, it comes with the territory. But to attempt this I needed advice on the azaleas, so I went looking and I kept seeing this name "Nucio" on azaleas in horticulture gardens. Finally, I found the Nucio brothers who've being raising azaleas for forty-five years, they're really the authority on them. They tell me it's going to work, so I'm going to live with the Nucio brothers. We had to mock-up the whole planting, full-scale, we had to grow them for a couple of years to get them to a scale at which they could be reasonably effective. You can really shape azaleas—it's a form the flower takes very nicely to. In fact, after you've done it for a while, the flower begins to look as if it's actually inlaid. It's an incredible form—the Japanese have been doing this for years.

The flower garden will be the *pièce de resistance* of the whole garden. I've been growing the plants up in Encinitas along with Jim Duggan. We've been growing all these plants and having a great time doing it, arguing and pissing and moaning about this and that. We've had a very, very tough year with the El Niño. It was almost foolhardy to plant a garden on a slope in a year when there's twice as much rain as there's ever been. A lot of our beautiful plants that we spent a couple of years raising were killed, and at times we had to start all over again. A lot of people say it is going to be very difficult just to try and water all these plants living next to each other. We have an incredible watering system but the garden will always require a lot of hands-on loving care. I have another three years to plant the garden and another seven years to finish the trees. The project's still very much in the making and obviously an incredible challenge and pleasure for me.

UNTITLED (FIVE THEMES)

Michael Benedikt

When Bill Stern called me and told me he wanted me to talk about art, architecture, and the future, I decided I had to set some limits on the topic. One of these is that I will not talk about virtual reality or cyberspace, but instead confine my remarks to architecture as built, to architecture as lived in, and indeed, to architecture as my first love. I want to thank Bob Irwin for stating many of the themes that I'm going to try to cover.

When asked to talk about architecture and art in such a broad way—actually when asked to talk about anything that isn't exactly what you're working on at the moment—it's inevitably like dropping a stone into a pond, the things one thinks of have a lot to do with what one has been thinking about at the time. For several years I have been immersed in the philosophy, psychology, and economics of value, raising questions such as: Why do things cost what they do? Why do people value what they do? How does our economy produce architecture, and how does our culture produce architecture? So it was a great provocation for me to talk about art, which seems to exist on the fringes of the economy. What I have to offer today is, I hope, food for thought and food for discussion. Having immersed myself in art for awhile, I named my talk *Untitled* and then proceeded to give it a title, which I call *Five Themes*. Now this would be suitably enigmatic, but I'm going to tell you now what those five themes are.

The first theme I've given the name *How the Arts Became the Performing Arts*. The second is called *Art's Relationship to Economics and Economic Life*. The third is *Art as the Capture and Redirection of Attention*. The fourth is called *The Ethical Dimension: Art and Architecture as Good Works*. And I'm going to conclude with *Glimpses of the Possible Future*. So here are the themes: performing art, economics, attention, ethics, and some glimpses of a possible future. These themes are of uneven and unequal length, some of them involve long bursts of slides, while others involve just listening to me drone on.

Let me start with the first, about art and performing art. It's always rather interesting to see how the popular press deals with art. Are they going to put it in the Entertainment section? Are they going to put it in the Living Arts section? Architecture itself generally floats around between those two, and sometimes Real Estate. People have a hard time actually placing architecture. They have an easier time placing art, because art is what happens in museums, art is what artists do. It also seems to me that the last immense involvement of the public with art was the Pop Art movement of the 1960s. Pop Art really did do what it set out to do, which was not only to be ironic and interesting about popular art, but to actually produce a level of meta-art: art about art, art about culture, art about what is popular. Through that process, the art itself became popular, outrageous, interesting, and really good to look at, scoff at, and shake your head at. It was extremely successful from a popular point of view, even though its protagonists were presumably being ironic and critical about the whole thing. I would also observe that art is mainstreamed in our culture, through such organizations as the National Endowment for the Arts, PBS and NPR. There's sort of an axis that runs through these organizations, and slowly but surely, it seems to me that our popular culture has abandoned the visual arts. Maybe this began as Pop Art itself waned. If you talk about "the arts," you generally mean the performing arts, i.e., opera, ballet, dance—things that are filmable and televisable, things that could be put on the radio. In fact, less and less of the NEA's budget goes to the visual arts; it's increasingly allotted to performance art. I would propose that this actually re-exerts a pressure back on artists and architects to begin to see themselves as performing artists.

Anyone in architecture school will tell you that if an architect is given a museum to build, the debate is always whether the museum should take a backseat to the art and present itself in as neutral a way as possible, or should the museum's architecture itself be of great interest? That has been answered by different museums in different ways. I'm asking a slightly different question, by proposing that architects are now starting to think of their architecture itself as performing. That is, an architecture which not only moves people around in balletic fashion, but an architecture that is itself frozen motion. An architecture which tries to capture human gesture and human poise. I would suggest that Frank Gehry's architecture is at the forefront of the idea of architecture as animate, as a performance in and of its own right. I would cite Gehry's Disney Concert Hall and Aerospace Museum, along with Bob Irwin's garden at the Getty as examples. I'd like to make a few comments about my experience of the garden. It's quite clear to me that the garden is almost something antithetical to the building. The sense of difference and opposition between the two in their attitudes toward performance is really extraordinary. I've never seen so much architecture devoted to so little art as at the Getty. The place is literally crawling with people, and it presents the same sort of view over and over again. I think it's amazingly courageous of Bob to say, "no view," and to turn the entire thing into a spectacular piece of art. I think there will be future debate as to which of these pieces actually wins, and I can tell you where my sympathies lie. So, after those observations, no big theory about the role of the metaphors of performance—whether they have a place in architecture, or when they do, how to handle that exactly.

The second theme is perhaps a little more difficult: art's relationship to economics and to economic life. When most of us talk about economic life, I think we have a rather narrow understanding of it. Economics is when you buy things for money, when money changes hands for things, and when things change hands for money or labor. It's highly involved with markets and prices. Economics as ordinarily understood penetrate almost everything we do and touch. It's a little harder to see that there's an economic trade, a sort of a barter that governs our social life in just the same way. For example, we will trade tokens such as compliments, favors, insults, acknowledgments of legitimacy, establishing oneself, and establishing someone else's legitimacy. We give each other permissions and trade permissions with each other. We offer each other security and other tokens of survival, so there's an entire economy of which money is a rather small part. Within the context of this larger understanding of social life as an economic engine, money itself is only one of the tokens that we trade, and we usually give it to each other for freedom. Now a lot of people are made unhappy by the idea that the laws of economics have a much broader application. I've always been intrigued by what disquiets us about extending economic hegemony over so much of our life. And the two areas where the subjection becomes loudest is in the relationship between economics and love, and the relationship between economics and art.

People do not want loving relationships to have even the slightest taint of economic trade associated with them. When you love someone, you do not do things for return. When you love what you're doing, you're not supposed to care how much you make doing it. Love is a great solvent of the rigid accounting and the precise expectations that we come to expect from economic life. So in loving relationships we actually seek refuge or relief from the economic. This works out most of the time, but we also know that loving relationships end; they can begin, so they can also end. When they do end, it's because the accounting has gotten a little rigid or a little brittle. Issues of fairness start to come forward. Issues of what I did, what you did, what you should have done, and what I should have done arise. You can be sure that when that begins, the actual essence of what is loving about that relationship has begun to wane.

It's far better to understand that there's an aspect of economics in loving relationships between people and families, and also between co-workers of companies, and so forth. Art finds itself in a similar situation. I think artists are in a very difficult relationship with economic life. On the one hand, artists must live, so they must be waiters or taxi drivers or some such thing, while they do their art for the love of art. What's more, they must usually decry all association with markets, galleries, buying, selling, and price making; they must act as though they do not care. But, of course, once an artist is accepted and once an artist finds a patron, the economic wheels begin to turn. This is true even though you're not going to hear a whole lot about it from podiums about art. Arthur Danto described the art world really beautifully in his significant book *The Transfiguration of the Commonplace*, where he shows that art is really, as Bob said, a constructed phenomenon, not only within the community of artists, but also within the larger community of collectors, gallerists, museum directors, critics from *Artforum*, and so on, down to the local newspaper. It is a very large and complex machine involving money, materials, and a huge number of compliments and insults. Being enmeshed in that system is what makes a work arrive at being read as art. And once it's enmeshed in that system, it is in an economic system involving money and tokens. Therefore, art is about the production of objects whose relationship to commerce is tenuous, a little like a satellite that hasn't quite been caught up in an orbital system. It waits and waits and at some moment it's swept into the system, and it becomes an economic object, an object that now has a value which will be speculated upon, bought, sold, jealously guarded, put in vaults, named, legitimized, etc. This means that the discourse of art and the discourses of love are often intermixed. They're often guarded in exactly the same way with very similar kinds of language. So you get books like Lewis Hyde's *The Gift*, a very interesting book in which the art object is posed as being part of a long lineage of gift giving. So the artist labors for no expectation of reward and simply donates the love of his work to society.

Without saying one way or another whether that's a valid or productive way to look at art, it is interesting to ask how architecture fits into this particular sort of relationship. Many architects will say buildings have to function, they have to meet budgets, and they have to be built on time; that's why they really aren't and can't be art. But architects also envy artists and wish that their work could also have a more fluid and edgy relationship with money, materials, and time. Architecture does have a critical apparatus (you might call it the arch world instead of the art world), in which buildings are published and praised or panned. But their ownership and their relationship to the economy are quite, quite different. In the final section of this little talk I will try to address how that might be adjusted to look more like art.

By the way, I don't very much like to distinguish between fine buildings and architecture. For me when a building gets good enough, it just gets to be architecture. I don't really go with the sort of division between a real nice building and architecture. A bad building can't be architecture just by trying to be cosmic. A really good building, which I would dignify with the name architecture, is a gift that keeps giving. Buildings never get tired of being good, and I think that's one of the most amazing and confounding things about buildings. It's a little unlike books, which have to be read to be good, or art, which has to be looked at to be good. A magnificent building—a building that is inspiring to look at and fun and comforting to be in—continues to be so without any further input except maintenance. And that makes them objects of particular interest. The work of the architect, in making an eternal or long-term good thing, is not reflected in how architects work, or how they are paid. I'd like to return to that. I would offer you a couple of images of what I think of when I think of buildings that are gifts that keep giving: the Caffé Florian in Venice and La Tourette.

I'd like to address a few remarks in an attempt to find what it is that makes art and architecture similar at the philosophical level. Art is the capture and redirection of attention. This has probably been the main theme of a lot of the talks we've heard this afternoon. It seems to me that art really has to do two things. It first has to capture your attention, and once your attention is caught, it has to redirect it away from what it is that caught your attention. An artwork performs that essential act. It's a little bit like bait and switch, except hopefully you switch to something better than what one was baited by. In classical art, attention is directed to the subject matter. The subject matter might be biblical, historical, documentary, or a landscape. But the idea is that what you see in that work of art, and what it is that holds you, does not redirect you away from that to yet something else. The subject matter, the painting, and the purpose of the painting are held to be superimposed upon one another. But starting with Impressionism—and I would say that for me this is really the essence of the modern project—art becomes more about the act of perception, about the techniques and the media of art, and about the artist's subjectivity. Following Duchamp, it's also about the legitimization processes of the art world itself. It's common for us to see that every artwork should be posed as a question or a challenge as to what art is. Art that does not ask the question, "What is art?" is, for us, somehow second-rate art, or, at least, certainly not avant-garde art. It was Duchamp who foregrounded the actual social legitimization processes that make art, and he made an art out of that very redirection of attention.

The other redirection made by certain types of art is towards a certain kind of feeling, and I think that both Irwin and Judd are exemplars of this redirection. This is the feeling that one is in the presence of ineffable authenticity. In my book *For an Architecture of Reality*, I called it the direct aesthetic experience of the real. By which I mean something that is unlike us, something that has to be, that cannot be taken back, that is not a mistake, that has presence, significance, materiality, and what I called emptiness. And by emptiness I meant two things: first, an absence of any desire to give a message, to deceive or to stand for something else; and second, in a more sort of Buddhist way, a feeling of attraction or draw, as in the way one is drawn into an empty room, or the way a fireplace without a fire suggests that a fire be built. This ineffable authenticity, the experience of something being absolutely real and not a mistake, is an experience that's been felt by many people for a long time. I would suggest that it goes back to when Moses saw the burning bush. I feel quite sure that the bush was not really burning, the bush was burning only with its own presence. What Moses saw quite clearly was simply the bush, the ineffable authenticity of that bush, and its final reality was all that he really had to see of God.

Art puts itself in the same position of precipitating that experience of absolute authenticity. I think that's what makes it close in many people's minds to the religious project. If I'm right about that, then we begin to see the art world that Danto describes—the artists, critics, galleries, collectors, museums, the whole machinery of it all—as a large and actually self-elaborating system. It will elaborate itself continuously; it's a system that arranges moments in which one knows that one is in the presence of something absolutely, ineffably authentic. It gets more and more difficult to do this, with every succeeding generation of art theory and every succeeding generation of artists. One is continuously drawn away from actually having that experience and yet the whole thing is yearning to precipitate that experience at the same time.

It's interesting to ask why this would become such a project. Why have we not been happy to look at dramatic paintings of great moments in history? Why have we not been in awe of human passion and suffering and representations of things that would make us better human beings? I can only surmise that it has to do with that old enemy we call the media. Because a lot of what art once did has been taken over by photography, film, television, radio, print journalism, and advertising. All of those media have taken the subject matter of art and, in their non-empty sense, turned it into things that motivate, things that will make you do things that you wouldn't otherwise have done. There are mechanisms in the direction of attention. For example, how does one learn about a museum show? I've seen billboards for museum shows—a curious place to find museum ads—I've also seen them on TV and in the newspapers. Anyone who directs a museum or a gallery knows that their first job is to fish for attention, then direct that attention to the building and the event. Once that's done, the architecture should refer directly to the art, and then once the art has captured your attention, you are finally redirected to the authenticity of the piece. In the final moment, the entire system of political arrangements and attention-getting tricks, whereby the moment is engineered, fall away, so that you can have two seconds of transcendence.

Pop Art in itself tried to solve this problem in an interesting way. It tried by embracing and amplifying the banal, so that one is faced with the underlying emptiness of it all. I take that to be Warhol's great invention, by embracing the banal he showed us the emptiness behind it. Minimalism has been a movement which I see as a mirror image to Pop Art, and it solves the same attention problem with a diametrically opposite move. It starts with the emptiness. That is to say the Minimalist artist knows full well that the person who is looking has come in off a busy street, has foregone watching TV, has driven a car, parked in a nasty parking lot, and has come to a purified and reduced environment. That very contrast is absolutely essential for the emptiness of a minimal moment.

The Pop elements are evident in this piece by Tom Otterness. It was done in 1989 or 1990, and it's a rather late example of what we can still recognize as Pop, yet the sense of distance and the irony is really beginning to show through. Pop is a movement that I still think has some life in it and it will be interesting to see where it goes.

More interesting in this context, however, is Donald Judd's work. I think Judd sensed that he needed to get to Marfa. He knew that for his Minimalist pieces to work they really had to be in a maximalist environment. He needed natural and changing light, greenery, old concrete, old buildings, and materials that had palimpsestic value. And he needed places like the artillery sheds, places with long, interesting, and intense social histories. He knew that these histories would be discussed and would deepen the experience of his aluminum structures. Of course, I think he was absolutely right and very sound in making that move.

Philip Johnson's Glass House executes a similar sort of motion within architecture. To state the obvious, this glass house would not look too good on a parking lot. It is not a building that takes command of its environment. It is a building, however, which is framed by its environment, and in this way it is able to reduce itself and rely on the principle of contrast.

In my book *For an Architecture of Reality*, I very optimistically and fondly prayed for a new kind of architecture, which I rather ambitiously called High Realism. What did I mean by High Realism? I think I meant the kind of thing to which Judd was directing our attention by his move to Marfa. That which is real around us is actually very poor at capturing our attention. That's one of the ironies of any kind of art or architectural form that says, "I'm going to be real." As was remarked earlier, it's like saying, "My work is about experience." Well, what isn't? If one's work is about being real, then one can't possibly fail since everything is real, including ideas, if you go far enough. So the qualifier "high" was an attempt to direct attention to the possibility of taking things that are real and amplifying that sense about them. But realism—high, low or medium-strength—is intrinsically very poor at capturing our attention. You walk past it all the time. Because of that, it takes a photographer or a certain kind of sensibility to be able to walk around the world and open yourself to accidents of composition, use, and history, looking for consciousness in a sense looking back at you.

Photorealism—which is a movement that intrigued me greatly—was beginning to do this. This is a work by Richard Estes. Photorealists quite frankly worked from photographs. They blew them up, put them on the wall, and spent six months painting them with a fine-hair brush. I thought, and still do think, it was an act of amazing artistic heroism, because it came so close to suicide. It's like getting into a plane, pointing it straight into the ground, and then pulling up only at the last moment, in the absolute faith that the artist has blessed the work by spending that much time on it, by the minute adjustments of their hand, and by the minute choices of color. In the attempt to be totally true to a photograph, they sort of pull off a monument to their humanity. I think the finest examples of Photorealism really achieve that. One of the side effects of what they did was this act of blessing the real and making what are essentially gigantic photographs. The Estes painting is about fifteen-by-nine feet. This work has much more resolution in it than any photograph could possibly have. That means he was actually inventing pixels as he painted. Some might argue that photography is the art form here, but it's an interesting ambition for architects to begin this kind of noticing, and to attempt to create buildings in and around which some photographer might pick up their camera, or a painter might sit down with an easel and a paintbrush. To create for others maybe by pointing out a direct aesthetic experience of the real.

In the break, I was discussing the influence of Zen Buddhism on mid-century art, and it seems clear to me that it has been an influence on both Judd and Irwin, and probably many others. But within Zen there's a wonderful saying which I will state now and maybe repeat again later. It says the following: "First there is a mountain. Then there is no mountain. Then there is." For me, that marks out a trajectory in which first there is a mountain, which is the ordinary perception of reality. Then there is no mountain, which is where one begins to doubt one's senses and one develops all kinds of theories and abstractions about what it is. It's a long journey for enlightenment and upon finding that enlightenment, one again re-embraces the ordinary and the real, which is now numinous for the intellectual journey. My hope would be that art might take this journey and watching Roni Horn's piece today gave me a lot of hope in that direction.

Let me go on to the fourth theme here. This is a very difficult area to talk about. It's the ethical dimension: art and architecture as good works. Earlier I talked about art as a sort of substitute for religious experience. It's often been remarked that the museum is like a modern temple these days, that's very old hat.

There's a categorical imperative that goes like this, shortened somewhat: "Act on principles that you would be happy to see everyone act on. Do things according to principles and maxims that you would be happy that everyone would do also." What it means is always be exemplary, because someone could be imitating you and someone could take your acts to be what they should do too. And if one thinks of any act as being universalized to everyone, then any act that went through that filter, so to speak, is sure to be ethical.

Philosophers will argue about this principle at length. I'd like to test it out as if it were kind of true, to simply put art through this particular little test. When I try to do that, what I come up with is: "Art is precisely that which cannot recommend itself for adoption as the norm." This is how art removes itself from the ethical realm. The artist is a person who precisely says of the categorical imperative, "this does not apply to me." Few artists will say that, in fact some artists will say, "No, go ahead and do what I do." But here's the kicker: it won't be very original. Deeply embedded within the discourse on art and architecture is the cult of originality. "If you copy me you will not be original." It also comes up in the idea of contextualism, a theory in architecture which enables the architect to be sort of original undercover. The architects says, "I can't possibly do anything that's ever been done before by anyone else, because this site is very flat and because this site also faces south." I would claim most contextualism is a subterfuge for architects longing to be totally original, not to repeat themselves or anyone else. Of course, there have been artists—Andy Warhol was probably one of the few and before him Duchamp—who deliberately went out and made repeatables. They made an issue of the fact that their work was just imitation, so to imitate them would be absurd. As with the photorealists, they said, "I am just taking a picture and I'm just painting it for a year. You can do that if you want, but it takes the kind of guts you don't have."

So when an artist moves from aesthetic statements to ethical statements, it's always a move from "be like me," "see as I see," or "act on principles that I act on." The artist who says these things has to be sure that if he were believed, it would be okay. Because if it's not true then that itself is actually a sham. The whole issue goes even deeper than this simple ethical principle. It almost goes to the level of the mathematical. When we count things, every time you count more than one—if you say two, three, four—in fact, I'm doing it. What is it there's four of, now five of? Fingers, right?

But as soon as I use the word fingers to count these on my hand, I am ignoring the uniqueness of this thumb, the uniqueness of this first finger, the uniqueness of the second, third, fourth. I am lumping them together, taking everything that makes them unique and tossing it out the window so that I can count them. If I say there are four hundred people in this room, that's true only insofar as you are all examples of people, or examples of individuals. But in fact, if I did not count you, I cannot go more than one for each of you without throwing away your uniqueness. And that is in fact something that Leibniz understood very well, called the principle of indiscernables, the identity of indiscernables. That which cannot be told apart, cannot be two things; that which can be told apart, cannot be counted without ignoring what it is that tells them apart. So art is deeply invested in resisting quantification, and also in reminding us that there is nothing of which there can be two.

This, in some sense, is one of the moral directions in art. If art resists quantification, it can also do it by rubbing our noses in it, which quickly has the same effect. And yet—and here's the irony—because it belongs to the art world, art depends critically on being classifiable, which means counted as a member of movement, direction or thought process. And this whole thing starts a game of cat and mouse between artist and the critic and collector, as the critic tries to pigeonhole and the artist runs away and refuses to be pigeonholed.

Finally, I'd like to offer some glimpses of the future. They really are glimpses in different sorts of directions. To go back to the issue of economics, I'm interested in the fact that artists, and especially young architects, will start by working for nothing. They have projects of intellectual interest to them, they have passions which no one else has, or for which they will spend inordinate amounts of time and labor getting off the ground. They hope that as their work begins to engage the real economy, they will be able to raise a family, feed them, put kids through college, do what they like to do. Who would not like to do that?

But the model that makes architects speculators in their own buildings has not been done, at least not by reputable architects. There are very few architects of intellectual quality and/or genius if you will, who will find a piece of land and say, "I know what would be nice on there," then design it, have it built, and take a chance. Perhaps this is the equivalent of an artist in a studio, stretching a canvas and saying, "I know what would be nice on there," and then spending a long time trying it out. When you hear in architecture school about working for a design/build firm or an architectural engineering firm, you generally hear, "Oh God, there goes art, there goes all of that." But if architects were more like artists, they would behave more like speculators. Ironically, the market for those kinds of buildings are a bit like the market for art, I believe the market would very soon start producing flowers of pretty wonderful architecture. In other words, architects need to start putting their money where their mouths are. There are, however, some laws which could be changed in interesting ways. In California there is a law, which maybe Bob could tell us about, called *le droit de suite*: the right of continuation. It's a law throughout Europe, but I think California is the only state to have adopted it. It states that every time a work of art changes hands, the artist has a right to a commission on the increase in value of that work. I'm not sure whether they take a hit if it loses value, but I do plan to look into it. This is a system that architects could easily get into: you make a building for little to no fee and you take an interest in it, either when it sells, or through the actual income generated by the building. This means you retire at fifty or sixty years old, because all of your children out there, your buildings, are sending income streams to you. It's another way of having architects invest their own creativity into a more artlike economic system.

Of course, this is not to say patronage in architecture shouldn't continue. In fact, the finest architecture in the world has been built with immense patronage. And one does actually wonder whether any market dynamic could ever simulate or re-create the benefits of patronage. I think we might try.

Finally, you may or may not know that tourism is the world's largest single industry. People are traveling more than ever. The interesting thing is that this trend makes the whole world a museum. This has interesting implications for architecture and for art, as it creates a renewed interest in the real thing, in the original, in the idea of ineffable authenticity. To some extent I think it accounts to some extent for the reason why Marfa will be a more visited place in the future. But the sights of tourism, such as Disneyland, and the sights where architecture is a performing art, both of these varieties of tourism—let's call the latter ecotourism or realist tourism, and the former unrealist tourism—both are actually flying apart. I wonder whether the middle ground will be left as banal as ever, and perhaps even larger in its scope.

My hopeful prediction for the future of architecture has to do with a combination of things. I hope, and to some extent I would predict, that there will be a renewed interest in classical principles of urban place-making in architecture, but this will not be the dead, old historicism made by guys in bow ties. It will be combined with an intensified interest in authenticity, in naturalness, and in health. I see a de-genderizing of interior design. I see the possibility for architects to suggest using fabrics in their buildings, as well as the use of sentiment, memory and luxury, all of which are conspicuously absent in modernism, which is basically a male movement and extremely macho. This is not to say that architecture won't keep the modernist love of strength, simplicity, excellence of detail, and an interest in natural light and materials. I have no idea why all of these things should not go together. I can also see—and would predict and hope for—an acceptance of a variety of cultures, the idea that style is not a dirty word, and the fact that class is not a dirty word. I would see it combined with a desire to create spaces and places of power without irony, to follow artists today in their attempt to connect powerfully to human emotion, and to content in their work. I would also hope and predict a willingness by architects to be imitated by anyone, that is, to use the test, "Would I be happy if everyone did this?" I would also hope that architects would always choose life over death.

Kingdome, Seattle, Washington, Compared to Floodburger, 1975, photo collage.

WHY RUN INTO BUILDINGS WHEN YOU CAN WALK BETWEEN THEM?

Claes Oldenburg and *Coosje van Bruggen*

CLAES OLDENBURG: This image is just by way of introducing the subject, we have on the left art, and we have on the right architecture. In the 1960s I began some designs for large structures in the city. One of the first was a proposal for a war monument in New York City, to be located at the intersection of Broadway and Canal Street. This is a major intersection between east, west, north, and south; and the war memorial would totally block it, making everything impossible. Another proposal was for London on the bank of the Thames River in 1966. The most remarkable thing about that time was the knee: the female knee had been revealed and it was very obvious everywhere. For some reason it appeared to be very unusual and shocking and deserving of a monument, and this was the result. Also in London, there was a proposal to place a toilet float in the Thames, next to the Parliament buildings. I've always been fascinated by objects. Once as a child, I opened the back of the toilet and I saw the float there. It struck me as very beautiful, it was a copper float. My idea here was to bring something big, beautiful, shiny and gold to the river; believe me, I didn't have any intention of making a satirical suggestion about the content of the river. You don't have to believe that, but that's how it is. When it comes to using objects there's a thing between myself and objects which is very difficult to explain. It goes far beyond the identity of the object and it has a great deal to do with the architectural char-

Proposed Colossal Monument, Victoria Embankment, London: Knees, 1966, photo collage.

acter of the object, because there are only a few objects that make themselves available to enlargement into architectural forms.

One other proposal was in London at Picadilly Circus, where I proposed replacing the fountain of Eros sculpture, which had been removed for repair. The idea was to place something more contemporary there, which would be tubes of lipsticks that would rise and fall with the coming and going of the Thames.

COOSJE VAN BRUGGEN: One way to avoid a lofty symbol and still achieve monumentality is through irony and the imagination. By replacing Nelson atop his column with a gear shift, a banal, everyday object becomes a substitution for the falseness of inflated patriotic sentiments usually connected with monuments. Another way to reach monumentality yet remain subversive and anti-heroic is to enlarge an object in scale. For example, the *Colossal Monu-*

WHY RUN INTO BUILDINGS...

Proposed Colossal Monument for Thames River: Thames Ball, 1967,
crayon, ink, watercolor on postcard.
Proposed Colossal Monument for Park Avenue, New York: Good Humor Bar, 1965,
crayon and watercolor.

ment for Park Avenue, New York: Good Humor Bar, 1965. The soft good
humor bar has become enormous and replaces what used to be the
Pan Am Building. There are many structural similarities. The bar is
built up of structural elements: rectangle, beam and circle—all
simple geometric forms, all applicable to architecture. The tunnel
at the base of the building coincides with the semi-circular bite of
the Good Humor Bar, so that the object becomes an architectonic
construction, while retaining its identity as an ice cream bar. The
thought of an ice cream bar rapidly melting and disappearing, as
if destined for consumption, is attractive, because sculptures not
only disappear in the reality of daily life, they also become dam-
aged and covered in graffiti. And many buildings erode over time.
This implies a threat not only to sculpture, but also to architecture. I've decided today to talk about neither art nor architecture,
but to try to see what art and architecture have in common.

CLAES OLDENBURG: After making these large proposals for objects translated into architectural scale, there came a proposition from the graduate students of architecture at Yale University, to commission a provocative monument that could be placed on the campus. At that time in 1969, there was no sculpture on the campus of Yale, in fact it was forbidden. This was also a critical monument: it was the time of the Vietnam War and co-education was about to begin at Yale. These two factors came together in the statement of the *Lipstick*, intended as a platform for speaking. When you had something to say, which many people did in those days, you were to climb up on the platform and, in the original concept, the lipstick was to be pumped up. It would rise like a telescope behind you as you spoke, then it would sink down, so that you had to keep pumping it to keep it up. When you were finished presenting your ideas, you stepped down and the next person would step up. This was placed in a very sensitive area, a highly architectural area in the center of the Yale campus, which is also a war memorial. The *Lipstick* stayed there for about a year until it was vandalized nearly to destruction. It was then removed and several years later it returned as an artwork, now placed in the Morse College. This is a rather nice situation, also very architectural, because it's in the context of a Saarinen design.

COOSJE VAN BRUGGEN: When the *Lipstick* was installed, the student paper asked Herbert Marcuse what he thought of the colossal monuments and the *Lipstick* at Yale. It's interesting to go back to 1969, the most subversive time on campus, and hear what Marcuse had to say:

> Strangely enough, I think that it would indeed be subversive. If you could ever imagine a situation in which this could be done you would have the revolution. If you could really envisage a situation where at the end of Park Avenue

Lipstick (Ascending) on Caterpillar Tracks, 1969/74, steel, aluminum, wood, painted with enamel; Yale University, New Haven, Connecticut.

there would be a huge Good Humor ice cream bar and in the middle of Times Square a huge banana I would say—and I think safely say—this society has come to an end. Because then people cannot take anything seriously. Neither the president, nor the cabinet, nor the corporate executives. There is a way in which this kind of satire, of humor, can indeed kill. I think it would be one of the most bloodless means to achieve a radical change. But the trouble is, you must already have the radical change in order to get it built and I don't see any evidence of that and the mere drawing wouldn't hurt and that makes it harmless. But just imagine that overnight it suddenly would be there.

And that's the problem for both architects and artists. One's vision, imagination, and creativity versus the reality of clients, programs, time, flowerpots, lantern posts, etc.—and you must try to make sense out of it all, or non-sense so as to subvert it.

CLAES OLDENBURG: The next step in the subversion of society was a sculpture that had been developed in connection to architecture, it became the first sculpture to be placed in a civic situation. The humble clothes pin is obviously a very architectural form. It was first used in an architectural context in 1967, when I made what I called a late submission to the Chicago Tribune architect competition, which was a very famous competition held to create a new building for the Tribune back in the 1930s. The building as you know is a Gothic structure in Chicago, and there's something about a clothes pin which is vaguely Gothic. I made a drawing which compared the two buildings and also proposed that this could very well be made into a skyscraper. The idea really came from flying into Chicago with a clothes pin in my hand, I held it against the window and I saw that it would fit very well somewhere near The Loop.

WHY RUN INTO BUILDINGS...

And then out of the shadows came a wealthy man who donated money for this project. It was placed not in Chicago but in Philadelphia, and it's located in what's known as the Center Square Project near City Hall. It's made of Cor-ten and it's about forty feet high with a stainless steel spring. It was placed in 1976, and there is a slight allusion to the number seventy-six in the spring, and there's a certain affinity with the Liberty Bell. Other than that, the site context, which became so important to us later, was not fully developed at this point. This was, however, the first sculpture that appeared in a city situation.

COOSJE VAN BRUGGEN: In 1976 Claes and I seriously began to speak about trying to leave the gallery system and venture out into the city to do large-scale urban projects. He had received his first GSA commission, the *Batcolumn*. This idea did not come out of the blue, because from the beginning Claes had really not cared much about being within the pristine surroundings of the museum. As a young artist in 1961, he had started his own store on the Lower East Side. From the beginning, the objects he displayed in this environment; the reality and the imagination; the private and the public; all came together. It was also here that his desire developed to get out into the city, and so he showed an oversized shirt, *Giant Blue Shirt with Brown Tie*, 1963, at a gas station.

I myself come from a generation of conceptual artists and in 1969, as a young assistant curator, I was very impressed by a show called *Square Pegs in Round Holes* at the Stedelijk Museum. It was the first time that conceptual artists such as Lawrence Weiner and Joseph Kosuth came to Amsterdam and participated in a show with artists such as Mario Merz and Jan Dibbets. And basically my attitude converged with Dibbets's, which was to dig up the foundation of the museum. I also felt very eager to get out into a different surrounding. We knew from the beginning that this would not be easy.

We felt this way because of the way sculpture was shown in museums. For example, Claes's *Three-Way Plug*, which is in front of the Oberlin Museum's new wing by Venturi. Basically the sculpture is shown in a way similar to George Washington on his pedestal in front of the New York Stock Exchange. It is a traditional way for an unconventional sculpture, so the only way to defend oneself is to try to find an environment where we might be able to add something different. Art in public places was absolutely the pits at the time. It was the worst. In Europe it was called *Kunst-am-Bau*: art attached to a building. It had no standing, the consensus was that you had sunk very low if you participated in this. So we decided that that was the way to go and so we took it on.

Of course we've had our own problems with architects. I remember very clearly an instance where Robert Venturi said to Claes, "I've always loved your art, and I've really enjoyed the *Three-Way Plug*. It would be wonderful as a vase on top of my building." As Theo van Doesburg said, "Sculpture should not lend itself to ever be a decoration of architecture."

So we decided to reverse the situation. We thought it was very practical to propose a museum wing in the form of the *Three-Way Plug*. Jacques Herzog showed us the incredibly huge, new Tate Gallery. There is never enough space and there will always be a need for new wings, so why don't we just plug one in? And each time you need more space, you plug in another. Actually, the way many architects think artists should behave is to make a little, nondescript sculpture on top of the site, rising timidly, not even as high as the first floor. This was the idea of the GSA architect at the site of the *Batcolumn* in Chicago. This produces nothing more than a turd on the sidewalk. We finally came to the conclusion much later that we should defend architecture, and we got the chance in 1998. At that time Claes had a show called *Bottle of Notes* in London. We were asked to participate by *The Independent* to contribute a proposal for London. At the time, Prince Charles had become notorious for

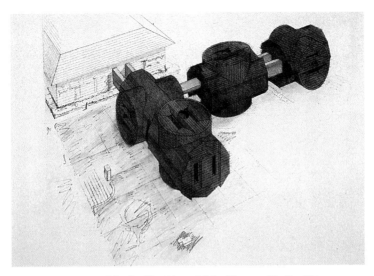

Alternative Proposal for the Allen Memorial Art Museum, Oberlin, Ohio, 1979,
hard and soft-ground etching with aquatint.

defending the real, traditional architecture of London. We decided
to make a proposal for One Poultry Street, which was to have an
office building on its corner. In the late 1960s Lord Palumbo asked
Mies van der Rohe to design a building, which Prince Charles
insulted by calling it "a glass stump." That was enough at the time
to discourage the construction of the building. I had read a little
text by Prince Charles about the state of architecture today. In it, he
mentioned that it was one of his rare opportunities to stir things
up, "to throw a proverbial royal brick through the inviting plate
glass of pompous professional pride, and to jump feet first into the
kind of Spaghetti Bolognese of red tape which cloaks this country
from one end to the other." So we decided to take him up on his
proposal. And here you see my foot in the Spaghetti Bolognese.

Architects are very interested in tall buildings. It seems to be a
competition about whose building is taller. Of course sculptors

Alternative Proposal for Number One Poultry Street, London:
Prince's Foot in Spaghetti, 1988, pencil.
Cologne, Germany.

have no chance to participate in this. In the context of scale, art
might be a porthole in an ocean liner, but it will have its own
effect. We are relegated to this situation. You see here the Cologne
cathedral, the clutter and the equestrian statue on its pedestal,
larger than life. This is the only scale at which the sculptor can
handle city surroundings. You see what we are up against—the
equestrian statue, the graffiti on the trains roaring by, the elec-
tricity poles, and the rails. Basically we are dealing with an impossible situation. Yesterday James Ackerman showed a slide of Judd's
concrete piece in Münster, full of graffiti. This is one of the most
difficult things in dealing with public art. A work on paper is
faster and better preserved than a public sculpture; the latter will
not endure time.

The question is, what lends itself to be placed on a pedestal, in
a time of not only toppling monuments but also toppling politi-

cians and toppling buildings? Sometimes buildings get reduced to arbitrary, meaningless sculptures. And sculpture is easier to move, which we've learned from *Tilted Arc*. But here we are, twenty years struggling in the city surroundings, hating pedestals and therefore slithering off them, as in our *Inverted Collar and Tie*, 1994, made out of fiberglass. Fiberglass is a material which allowed us to make soft sculpture in a hard city surrounding, at the entry-level of the building. Buildings don't move, but the sculpture has a dynamic quality, it's part of the street, it stands in front of the building and yet it tries to get away from it. That is our reality.

CLAES OLDENBURG: The important thing for us is not really an antagonism between art and architecture, but more of an interchange. A recognition that we are in the same space, that we are both building against gravity, and that in the end there may be quite a bit of similarity between us. Frank, Coosje, and I often discuss what the real differences between art and architecture are. They may be as simple as the fact that art does not have windows or toilets. In fact, art doesn't have much of an interior. But even that—as you'll see later on with the binoculars—even that is something that we've tried to overcome.

Going back a few years to the *Batcolumn* in Chicago, this was the first piece in 1977 that Coosje actively collaborated on with me, and she selected the color. There was a very good reason for the color. Chicago is probably the most important architectural city in the United States, at least in legend. I grew up there and I was aware of all of the buildings, and from time to time I would walk around and look at the buildings by bending forward and looking through my legs, as Thoreau recommended. After a while, because of perspective, they all seemed to assume a kind of bat-like shape. This translated into a structure over one hundred feet high, which was known as the *Batcolumn*. Now that's very important because Chicago has been obsessed with columns ever since its beginning.

Louis Sullivan was rejected for the World's Fair of 1893, as Neo-Classicism came in and took his place. Every building in Chicago worth anything had to have a column. So the column is a very ingrained thing, just as baseball is. Although they have teams that never win, people go all the time, they love baseball. We wanted to have something which was a quasi-architectural structure, something which did not assert itself so much as an object, but which used the object as a way of contacting the architecture.

The *Batcolumn* is in front of the Social Security Building and the structure of it picks up on the fire escapes, the water tanks, and especially the elevated structure that is so characteristic of The Loop. What was interesting about this site is that when we put it up, it was west of The Loop in a rather seamy section known as Skid Row. It gives you an insight into site-specificity in that a few years later, this whole area was completely transformed architecturally. Originally there were Skid Row places and empty lots surrounding it. Today an enormous Helmut Jahn building rises behind it, with many other skyscrapers around it. Even more than when it was placed, it fulfills its relationship to the architecture around it.

Another column form which was developed in 1981 was the inverted *Flashlight* for the campus of the University of Nevada at Las Vegas. We all have the association of light with Las Vegas. It's the most conspicuous thing there, you spend most of your time at night in the company of lights. So the flashlight seemed to be a perfect structure, and also a very classical structure. The outside was black, and at that time there was hardly anything of that color in Las Vegas, everything was white. I understand they've since built a pyramid in black which I haven't seen, but at the time the absence of color was very important to our subject. We created a form that has deep space in it, so it's even darker than dark, because it captures the shadow during the daylight and it's always intensely black. At night there's a pool of light under it. The *Flashlight* is standing on its head, and there's a kind of a rim of light at

Batcolumn, 1977, steel column, aluminum base, polyurethane enamel;
Chicago, Illinois.

Flashlight, 1981, steel, polyurethane enamel;
University of Nevada, Las Vegas.

the bottom which is a very subtle light, which is intended to be a contrast to the garish lighting of the strip.

We were naturally inspired by some of the architecture in Las Vegas, much of which no longer exists. Structures there are reaching up, and we thought that's another thing we wanted to oppose, so our *Flashlight* faces down. We were also very involved with the nature of Las Vegas, which is something you don't always see in the casinos. We spent a lot of time walking among cactuses and the cactus element crept into the column through the shape. Another ingredient was a little lighthouse that stands on an island in the East River in New York, which is a very secret place. Very few people know about this, it's quite a romantic place to visit. You go over the bridge to what used to be known as Welfare Island, it's now Roosevelt Island, and you go to the northernmost point and there you find this little lighthouse. Our *Flashlight* is in a way based upon this.

WHY RUN INTO BUILDINGS...

When we make a sculpture in a site we not only try to relate to the forms that exist there, we also try to pick up some kind of an ethos or an unconscious current, which is usually expressed in stereotypes and in what people say and how they behave. We try to bring this together with our own personal sensations. We've always maintained that what we are doing is private art in public places. It's a kind of mixture of our perceptions and what we imagine are the perceptions of others, which are also perceptions that can be developed over time. Unlike the things that you see in museums, these sculptures are there every day, when you go to work and when you come home. You pass this thing every day and you have time to reflect on it, and to put things into it. And after a while, if we have done our job right, it becomes a part of the community. People begin to use it as a sort of emblem, and they speak about it as if it's theirs. It starts with a rejection, because we always come in with something that's rather strange. We don't mean to cater to the community, so we come in with something that they've never seen before, but after a while they become accustomed to it.

COOSJE VAN BRUGGEN: Our large-scale projects are a combination of imagination and reality. Yesterday, James Ackerman said that the intentions of the artists are not part of a sculpture, or at least one should view the sculpture without knowing the intentions of the artist. However, I think that today architects and artists have very specific ideas and intentions. Yes, it's true a sculpture or a building has to be seen by itself autonomously, but at the same time the idea of an historical, linear development has broken down. We no longer have one movement following the next, and I'm sure that every architect and every artist tries to avoid becoming a trademark. I know that Donald Judd was an artist who would express his ideas very particularly about what his sculpture and his architecture were about. This went beyond a movement and beyond historical analysis. I think that that is what we are up against each time an artist, sculptor, painter or architect starts out: he or she is pinned down to what is expected from him or her, and very soon one becomes a trademark. I know that Roni Horn is one of those artists who manages not to be restricted to a trademark. Each time we go into a situation, we try to come up with a very specific idea to that given situation. In order to do so, we go to the site and we listen.

At the University of Pennsylvania, we were asked to cover up a monstrous wall on the campus. We knew that we couldn't do that and it irritated us. Why should we cover up the mistakes of not only the architect, but also the ones who had commissioned this wall? We didn't want to do that, so instead we found our own place and we made what we call an obstacle monument. We tried to find the most discarded object on the campus. And our idea was a *Split Button*, which the students have to walk around and experience on their way to class. We hate pedestals, so we put the sculpture as an obstacle monument on the ground. The great advantage of doing a modest piece is that one can give it an emotive quality and a certain kind of drama, as James Ackerman said in his lecture yesterday. We are very aware of these things, and while we try to stay detached and give it a cool appearance, we hope to get to an emotive quality at the same time, which turns the work into something more than just a sculpture put in front of a building.

By accident I found a little book by Jorge Luis Borges called *Atlas*. Borges, who was nearly blind at the time, visited the university and he had found our sculpture. In the meantime our sculpture had become a symbol for the students, and they had begun to use it in any way possible. It was used as a memorial for students who had died of AIDS. And it was the site for the football team's photo. Artists, writers, and architects all work with image banks, each one has his own images in his head, associative images. I know that Frank Gehry—and also Don Judd—spoke in images many

Split Button, 1981, aluminum, polyurethane enamel;
University of Pennsylvania, Philadelphia.

times. As a writer, Borges could better state what our sculpture was about than we ever could have done. He wrote:

> I'm quite sure that Mr. So-and-so whose name I can no longer recall, saw something at a glance, that no one had ever seen before since the beginning of history. What he saw was a button. He saw that everyday artifact that so engages the fingers and he understood that in order to transmit this closure, the revelation of something so simple, he must augment its size and execute the vast and serene circle we see at the center of a square in Philadelphia.

The *Split Button*, with its four equal holes, represents the ground plan of Philadelphia, so it even has an architectural connotation.

Obstacle monuments are one of our favorite ways to participate within a surrounding. In Parc La Villette in Paris we were asked to contribute a sculpture in a park ordered by the red follies of Bernard Tschumi and the furniture of Phillipe Starck. We decided to project the configuration of a bicycle, not taking into account the architectural order of the place. We let it come up wherever it would lead us. So the handle with the bell is very close to a path, the seat is within the grass and so on. Everything falls in place, but it is a different type of order, imposed upon the architect's order, and yet it seems to work. Creating these obstacle monuments and pushing the parameters of sculpture creates something of a danger. For example, when one puts a bronze, equestrian horse on a pedestal, everybody knows it is a sculpture. The difficulty today is that we don't live in the nineteenth century, and art is a very marginal part of our society. So our problem in creating an obstacle monument, with its tactile surface, is that it gets confused with playground sculpture. And the irony of fate in this situation is that the follies are supposed to be the playthings for the children, and the sculpture is not supposed to be touched. However, in this case, the reality is the other way around. The follies are not being used and our sculpture is very often a part of an education in how to climb a mountain.

CLAES OLDENBURG: In this case we were working with the architect Edward Larrabee Barnes who had designed a garden for the Walker Arts Center. We were asked to come up with something which would be a focus of the rather symmetrical walk past some outdoor rooms that he had created for sculpture. We wanted to create something which was a focus, but at the same time didn't dominate. So we wanted a form that was lying down. I'd been playing with a spoon for a long time, trying to make it into a sculpture. It hadn't succeeded until one day, when we were thinking about this project, Coosje said, "Why don't you put a cherry in the spoon?

Spoonbridge and Cherry, 1988, aluminum, polyurethane enamel, stainless steel; Walker Art Center, Minneapolis, Minnesota.

That's what it needs. The spoon itself is a rather dull masculine object, but if you put some life into it and some color maybe we'd have something."

So that was the starting point, and the cherry went in. Then the cherry developed into a sprouting fountain that sprayed water out of the top, then ran down the sides of the cherry and into the spoon, then into a pond that Coosje designed in the middle of the area. Perhaps in the end we did dominate that part of the field, but it's a very subtle fountain. We have dealt with fountains, but we find that we want to keep the activity of the water usually rather limited. But in this case, it does create a very glossy cherry.

Another rather distant collaboration with Edward Larrabee Barnes was the *Stake Hitch* for the Dallas Museum. Barnes created this very high barrel vault which was difficult to fill with anything like artwork. So the museum came up with a rather daring plan to

Stake Hitch, 1984, stake: aluminum steel, epoxy, polyurethane enamel;
rope: polyurethane foam, plastics, fiberglass-reinforced plastic, latex paint;
Dallas Museum of Art, Texas.

make this room into a rather special room, and they commissioned five or six artists to do large pieces. Ours was the first to be installed, and the *Stake Hitch* penetrates into the receiving room below. So the workers in the museum have half of the sculpture to themselves. It's kind of a cachet actually to be allowed to go down there and look at the point. Not everybody's seen it, but if you're in Dallas and in the museum, just ask them to show you the rest of the sculpture. The rope goes up to the ceiling and then out into some imaginary creature which Don visualized. On the other side there's a mural by Sol Lewitt, but that was as far as they got with this plan to make the room special, so there are only two large projects realized. The room is now used for changing exhibitions, which is a pity.

In Weil am Rhein, outside of Basel, there's a very unique company called Vitra, a manufacturer of contemporary chairs and

Balancing Tools, 1984, steel, polyurehtane enamel;
Vitra International, Weil am Rhein, Germany.

furniture. We were asked by the owner of the factory, Rolf
Fehlbaum, to create a sculpture for his father's seventieth birth-
day. We created something we called the *Balancing Tools.* We did
this because we wanted to emphasize the rather inventive, hand-
made quality of the original products they were manufacturing.
Many of the chairs and furniture at that time were designed by
Charles and Ray Eames. They had a thing about special tools and
about the simplicity of tools; we wanted to go back to the beginning and do a kind of homage to that. Rolf had ambitions to bring
art and architecture together in a very original way, and he commissioned other sculptures and other architects, among them
Frank Gehry, who created his fantastic and wonderful chair museum, which you see in the background. It's a structure of tilting
planes and walls and we'd like to think that the dance that the *Balancing Tools* are doing reflects what's going on in the building. I

don't know if everyone will agree with this, but we feel that this is one of the unique cases where sculpture and architecture are playing together.

COOSJE VAN BRUGGEN: This is an instance where we were asked to enliven a very heavy, Neo-Classical museum building. The difficulty with landscape projects is that monolithic sculpture will not work on a huge field. The Nelson-Atkins Museum is a very strong Neo-Classical building, nearly a fortress, with a huge field in front lined on both sides with Henry Moore's sculptures. We were asked to come up with a sculpture that would not go over the middle axis of the field. In the first idea at an earlier instance, Claes had been asked by a committee to do a sculpture, and he had proposed giant pool balls running down the field. This created such a passion that one trustee said to another, "If you allow this on our field, I'll kill you."

This museum felt so heavy that when we arrived, I had to sit on a bench, and I fell asleep for a moment. When I looked up, I saw a painting of an Indian with a headdress, and I said to Claes, "What about some huge feathers, just dropped on the field?" This really characterizes how we work, because the pool ball and the feather came together into a different structure: a shuttlecock. We realized that we could have more shuttlecocks in different configurations, that it could be a classical vase or a teepee, and we scattered them over the field.

All of this is leading up to the relation of art and architecture. During the anthology show, Thomas Krens asked us to do a site-specific work for the Guggenheim. We perceived Frank Lloyd Wright's building as a public space in the central atrium, with a marginal ramp situation around it, a kind of centrifugal proposition. I had read a remark by Frank Lloyd Wright that organic architecture should be like a wildflower found along the roadside. Looking up into the atrium, we realized that the glass cupola is basically like

Shuttlecocks, 1984, aluminum, fiberglass-reinforced plastic, polyurethane enamel; The Nelson-Atkins Museum of Art, Kansas City, Missouri.

the soft feathers of a shuttlecock. So we created the *Soft Shuttlecock*, and the great advantage of the feathers was that we could show the great, multi-directional tendency of this building. Not only the verticality, but also the horizontality of the building became more apparent.

By the way, this idea of trying to bring verticality down to horizontality was a favorite of Donald Judd. I remember clearly visiting him one day, he was complaining about the World Trade Center in New York. He said to me, "I have a different proposal, why don't we lay them down in the Hudson River and then, at least, I would have my view." Don always dealt with horizontality. We were asked once by Frank Gehry to do a project for Peter Lewis in Cleveland. Frank will surely tell it better than I do, I just hope he will. Frank made a skyscraper relating to the skyscrapers in Cleveland, and Don came in with a completely alternative proposal, stating that Cleveland basically had to be brought back to the Burnham plan, which means four squares and horizontality. It is, I think, the vision of each of us that is the most interesting. Not the vision in itself, but the development of language and the insistence upon it, and then attempting to live with other visions. That is what we tried to do with the Guggenheim. The same sculpture was shown in Bilbao, and everybody said it was beautiful. Yes, it may have been beautiful, but it wasn't installed by us and we would have done it differently. We would have brought the piece out more into the space, because Frank's spumous columns and our organic *Soft Shuttlecock* do indeed have something in common. It means that while one keeps one's own identity, there is the possibility to interact, to cross over. I think that that is extremely valuable, because in working with Frank, we've unlearned habits and jumped into new ventures. Crossing over from art to architecture is actually very dangerous. The other way is very dangerous too. Because each has its continuation and each has its breaking point, there is a point you don't want to cross. There is a situation where

WHY RUN INTO BUILDINGS...

you are seen as very traditional in one field, while you could be very radical in the other, and it is this tension that really attracts us.

CLAES OLDENBURG: Well, you know that this piece is sitting out in the field here. You know that it was made for the field, and perhaps you heard something about how it came about: finding a horseshoe on the road and developing that into the monument to Louis. But perhaps what you didn't know is that we tried it out first in New York. The Seagram Building—or what used to be known as the Seagram Building on Park Avenue—has a plaza in front of it, and from time to time sculptors are invited to show for brief periods there. Before it came to Marfa, the horseshoe, *Monument to the Last Horse*, was placed in this site during the summer of 1991. It actually worked in the site. The color went with the Mies building, and it also gave a kind of life to the façade, which was even more than we expected. Then it traveled across country to where it really belonged, a place with no skyscrapers, or a place where the skyscrapers are all lying down. The horizontality of this place is probably one of the things that appealed so much to Don. I remember that we were driving with him from his ranch, and there's a kind of a slope that begins far away, so that you can see the town of Marfa in the distance for about one-half hour before you actually arrive. It's just one level plane all the way. The nice thing about this piece is that if you get up early in the morning, about 5:30 or so, you can catch the sun rising in the center of the "C." It's nice to have a sculpture that you can actually go out and touch. So I hope that you've been out to visit it.

One of our most recent works is also very involved with architecture. This is in Japan, in front of a convention center in a new section of Tokyo that lies across the Rainbow Bridge. It's a section where the architecture is very unusual and very powerful; we needed a structure that could compete with the architecture, so

Monument to the Last Horse, 1991, aluminum and polyurethane
with polyurethane enamel; Chinati Foundation, Marfa, Texas.

the *Saw, Sawing* is conceived as sawing through the ground. *Saw, Sawing* has a soft, organic handle in the color of red, which is totally different from anything in its surroundings. This place is really a masterpiece and a nightmare of a building—it's one of the biggest buildings I've ever seen. It has passages and escalators and elevators and so on, and the saw stands there in a mysterious presence, because you realize there's nothing like this saw in Japan. When we do structures for other countries, it's sometimes a little difficult to talk to the people or to understand exactly what's on their mind. This is especially true in Japan. The Japanese who commissioned us did not want us to try to do that. They wanted to have something which represents our culture, at least that's what we were told. We think *Saw, Sawing* is a very successful piece because of it's mysteriousness in its Japanese location. Not everyone quite knows what it is, yet we know what it is, and so it has a kind of dou-

WHY RUN INTO BUILDINGS...

Saw, Sawing, 1996, fiberglass-reinforced plastic painted with polyester gelcoat and polyurethane clearcoat, steel, epoxy resin, urethane and PVC foams; Tokyo International Exhibition Center, Japan.

ble identity. The top part is made of fiberglass, we worked with a factory that specializes in architectural work. This is another thing that binds us to architecture, we use many of the same techniques in realizing these works, so we have to think architecturally. The hope had been to build the thing entirely out of fiberglass. We had a state-of-the-art technology but the Japanese had building codes which forbid that, and so there is a very strong internal structure of steel. Building codes are one of the things that relate us very much to architecture.

COOSJE VAN BRUGGEN: I have the pleasure to introduce the next speaker. In 1984 Claes, Frank Gehry, and I worked with graduate students of architecture at the University in Milan. This resulted a year later in a performance called *Il Corso del Coltello—The Course of the Knife,* held outdoors at the Arsenale in Venice. Besides being a parody on the *commedia dell'arte*, *The Course of the Knife* dealt with the contending forces in Venice: the present versus the past, art versus kitsch, consumerism versus authenticity. It featured a ship combining the souvenir Swiss Army Knife with the ceremonial oar-propelled *bucintoro* of ancient Venice. The ship's mast, a corkscrew, was flanked by two folding blades. This contradictory combination of a screwing element with two sharp blades could serve as the definition of an artist. It turned out also to be the definition of an architect.

Each protagonist assumed two personas: an ideal one relating to the history of Venice; the other, debased, situated in its present. At the same time the roles were autobiographical, and I had the pleasure to write a scenario for the characters.

Claes Oldenburg, alias Dr. Coltello, alias Marco Polo, played a decadent souvenirs peddler and also a Sunday painter, who loved to paint upside down. It was a satire on his own beginnings, in which he pitted his imagination against the reality of a mercantile society, by opening his *Store* on the Lower East Side in December, 1961. Accompanied by his statement: "I'm for an art that doesn't sit on its ass in the museum."

Georgia Sandbag, a combination of George Sand and Calamity Jane, started out as a travel agent and now has the pleasure to travel herself and write notes in her diary.

Frank O. Gehry, dressed in a costume of architectural fragments and a fish-faced Fedora, was Frankie P. Toronto, a barber from Venice, California; trying to satisfy his mobster clientele. In his admiration for classicist architecture, he aspired to be Palladio, while at the same time he cut and sliced away at the old order, to let the new one unfold.

Frank gave a lecture about fat architecture, don't ask me why, but it was quite amusing. Soon after, we began to talk about starting to do more things together. One of the principles which we both applied to our work was the idea of disorganized order.

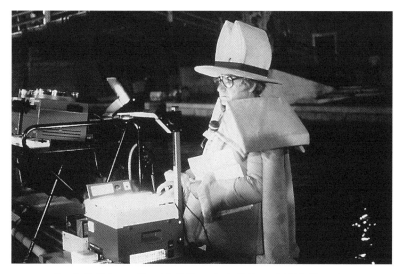

Frank O. Gehry as Frankie P. Toronto in *Il Corso del Coltello,* 1985;
Venice, Italy.

The one true attempt at collaboration occurred when Frank was
commissioned to do a camp for children with cancer in the Malibu
mountains. Our layout of the camp was guided by this principle of
disorganized order. In trying to find a connecting theme, we
thought about a tidal wave. We were totally moved by these children, who, despite their disease, had such a zest for life that they
nearly ignored it. We felt that we should try to do something that
would give them an extraordinary experience, and we knew that
some of them had a short time to live. So we wanted this to be a
camp where parents could come with their children and stay for a
while. There would be an infirmary but it would not be removed
from the location of daily activities, because we wanted all children to be able to participate at all times. Our first attempt at
something together was a dining hall in the form of a receding
wave, which is cut and sliced, with a porch in the form of a ship in

Binoculars, 1981, steel frame, concrete and cement plaster painted with elestomeric paint; Chiat/Day Building, Venice, California.

front. The kitchen was a milk can. Unfortunately, we never got the chance to really work the idea out. But I do remember that Frank, Claes and I were sitting at the table and each of us was very nervous, and it was very hard to know how we were going to work together. We felt inhibited because it's not about being clever or trying to do something that is already confirmed. This was an idea and at the same time it was a move where we had to be vulnerable. We had to try to jump into unknown territory, while still taking into account each other. That is what true collaboration is about. It's most difficult to not be inhibited, to throw out stupid thoughts, because maybe being stupid leads to an unconventional track, which will provide a chance to do something new. The children's camp was the perfect metaphor for us to try and do something together.

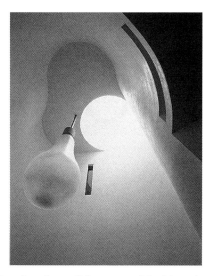

Interior of one of the rooms of the binoculars
showing light bulb and slit window.

While we worked on the performance in Venice, we had another project with the same architectural students. This was to come up with a neighborhood on the backstage of Venice. Claes made a binoculars theater, and all three of us worked on it. Of course this idea of making a neighborhood would never become reality. However, Frank had a model of the binoculars on his desk. One day we got a phone call from him. He'd had a meeting with Jay Chiat, and they both felt that the facade of the Chiat/Day Building was unresolved. The model of Claes's binoculars were on Frank's desk and he was just trying to show Jay that the facade needed something else. He put the binoculars in his facade, and they both thought maybe that would be it. We thought Frank was out of his mind, this was the most generous gesture we could imagine. How does an architect even consider the thought of giving part of his facade to a sculptor? Well, Frank did that, and he's regretted it ever since.

The biggest problem is that when one makes a book, it's usually vertically oriented, so the two parts of Frank's building are always cut off, but the binoculars are always there. But that's not our fault.

This is the interior. You can see a slit, that's the window. Frank Gehry told us you have not made architecture unless you put in a window. This, of course, destroyed the beautiful curve of the binoculars, but we found a place inside the column. It's hardly visible and the enormous light bulb in the interior obscures it anyway.

CLAES OLDENBURG: I guess that we've come to the end, right? The fact is that this was the only sculpture that we made that has an interior. But we were completely unable to find a function for it, and to this day there's nothing in there but the light bulb. I think that's one of the problems for its future.

FRANK GEHRY: The idea room.

CLAES OLDENBURG: The idea room. Yes, that's what we thought. You go in there if you have no ideas.

RECENT WORK

Frank Gehry

Don Judd hated my work. We liked each other though, we were friendly to each other and we tried to work together a few times, and I truly respected his work. It was a little difficult to come here.

My relationship with artists started very innocently. I started my practice in L.A., and when I built my first buildings the architects started making bad noises against me, while the local artists started saying nice things. So guess where I went?

I had some education in art history and a big, big, big love affair with painting. It's something I've placed on the highest pedestal of human activity, and so I've never dared try it myself. I've always fantasized that the moment of truth for a painter is facing the white canvas; the same moment of truth comes for an architect after you've solved all the budget problems, the contextual problems, the relationship with gravity, and all of the things that you have to do to make a building. You're finally left with choosing the formal relationships: the shape, form, materials, and color. I've always thought that it was the same moment of truth, and I found that to be true when I did collaborate with my friends.

This little studio was one of my first buildings in L.A., built in 1964 for Lou Danziger, a graphic designer. He was kind of an artist. He wanted a studio for his graphic design company, and as soon as it was built he bought a pool table, became a pool expert, and forgot about graphic design.

The Los Angeles County Museum brought all of these people together on the steps of the museum—that's me with my mustache, there's Lou Danziger, my client; that bald head is Claes Oldenburg. There's Ed Ruscha, Esther McCoy, Judy Chicago, Cesar Pelli, Lloyd Hammerall, Tony Berlant, John Altoon, Billy Al Bengston and Rudy Genreich, Larry Bell, Ed Kienholz, and Craig Kaufman. There's John Coplans, who would later undress and reveal himself to all of us. It was at that time that Claes was working in L.A. Of course he only turned his back to me, he never really talked to me. But he was doing the proposal for the new Pasadena Museum of Art, and he was very presumptuous in that he didn't like what the architect was doing, so he decided to make his own proposal, which was a can of tobacco with a screw. It would have made a better museum than the one they built. Because I was the only architect hanging around the art scene, he asked me to do the working drawings for this building and make it real. I agreed to do it, but he never called back.

In New York somebody is always imagining things for architects to do, for which they won't get paid. They asked a bunch of people to collaborate on whatever, and Richard Serra and I collaborated on a bridge between the Chrysler Building and the World Trade Center. I was starting my fish fetish at that time, so I decided to make a building that looked like a fish out in the water, and Richard made a big plate. I got very involved with the windows because architects have to design windows. That's the difference—the goddamned windows screw up the sculpture—that's what happens. So I made a fish scale window for this building, and these represented the floors of the building, etc.

I like doing furniture because architecture takes too long to build. I started making stuff out of cardboard and Bob Irwin—who is one of the neatest people I've ever had the opportunity to spend time with—used to hang around and talk to me at the time. I was designing boxy stuff that Don Judd probably would have liked, and

Danziger Studio and Residence, Hollywood, Los Angeles, California; 1964/65.

Bob Irwin designed this chair. I got really jealous and got into it, and started to do all these things. We had a fun relationship on this, except I guess Bob discovered that little laid-back Frankie, who pretended to be a pussycat, actually had a big ego. He got scared.

I was fascinated with the issue of denial in society. I think we all are aware that we don't deal with it much. A material like chainlink fencing is made in such great quantities and is absorbed by the culture worldwide, yet it remains one of the most despised materials made on the face of the earth. But everybody has it and uses it. Houses in Bel Air have big chain link fences around their entries in the form of a tennis court—they become a symbol of wealth, and people don't think of them as chainlink. My friend Bob Irwin had been working with scrim pieces that were ephemeral, beautiful, and beyond belief. When I started playing with the chainlink that's where I went. I understood the work that he had done, and I understood the applicability of it to what I was trying to do.

At Loyola Law School the students wanted something that represented a symbol of the law. It was a very low budget project, and the only thing I could come up with was a few abstract columns, which were supposed to somehow represent the legal profession. I had a column laying on the floor just to somehow represent imperfection in the legal profession, but the lawyers wouldn't let me do it. Years later Claes and Coosje came back and corrected the problem for me by building a fifth column that represented all of those things and incorporated my chainlink. This chainlink ain't ordinary chainlink, it's in perspective, so it's very complicated. I learned a lot from this building and from these shapes, because at this point I hadn't ventured into this area of the fold. It's an area that I love so much in Klaus Sluiter and in Bernini, in great sculpture that I revere and enjoy. It was only after Claes and Coosje made *Toppling Ladder with Spilling Paint* that I started to play with it.

In the building for Peter Lewis in Cleveland, the original story is that Peter Eisenman had designed a horizontal building, and Peter Lewis asked me to bring some of my artist friends in to collaborate. I brought in Claes and Coosje, Don Judd, Carl Andre, and Richard Serra. It was a very important presentation. Peter Eisenman presented this crazy, horizontal, broken surfaced building, then Don came in with his ten little boxes—he was supposed to collaborate, but he made a counterproposal. So Peter got a little pissed off and went to the ball game, leaving me to deal with Judd. It was the discussion that Don and I had, recorded on videotape somewhere, that I remember as a very beautiful interaction, at least from my point of view.

I knew this project was never going to get built, I knew it was just folly time. So when I was given the front and center, I put it up in the air because I'd never done a high-rise. Then I asked the artists to come and play. The first thing Claes and Coosje did was take a paper bag and put it over the top of the building, letting all of the bag's contents sort of roll down the side. I backed them off from that. Judd was going to do this flat plate out onto the lake. Carl Andre was going to do a reflecting pool, and I forget what Richard Serra was going to do. I think he got mad and went home. Claes and Coosje put the Cleveland Plain-Dealer on the roof, and they did a C-clamp for Cleveland, clamping one of the parts of the building to the parking garage.

About the issue of my ego, I knew that the pictures were going to be what they were, and I did have a moment of pause, but when I did see the pictures of the binoculars on the cover of my friend Charlie Jenck's book, I didn't even realize I wasn't in it. I was so prepared for it, I call it the Binocular Building and I've sort of subsumed it into my life. In fact, I even think I did it sometimes.

When they were passing out the museums in L.A., they passed over me a little. They gave me the fallback position, an old police warehouse, which we turned into what is affectionately known as

Temporary Contemporary, Los Angeles, California; 1982/83.

the Temporary Contemporary. The only reason to show it is the fact that we're always trying to make things so simple for art. But having logged a lot of time in artists' studios over the years, I realized that the art looks really great in their studios. It's very complex, the ceilings are filled with structure, and there's all kinds of stuff all around, but it works. It seems like the issue is how ordinary the stuff is. If it's not contrived, if it's left ordinary, then it doesn't become fussy detailing. We followed that logic, we didn't have money to do anything else, and it really was an enlightenment for all of us. Within the same space I collaborated with Lucinda Childs and the composer John Adams and brought chain-link again into the mix.

The first real museum I did is in Minneapolis and it's modest—eight million dollars. The facade is where the offices and conference rooms are located, it faces the Mississippi River. The views up

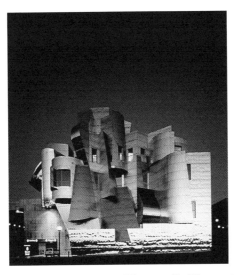

Frederick R. Weisman Art Museum, Minneapolis, Minnesota; 1990/93.
Museum at sunset.

and down are better than the frontal views. I made a corrugated facade, and then I started to manipulate into it. I covered it with shiny stainless steel when I realized it was facing west, so every day we would get this wonderful present from nature.

The inside is clean, it's a big open space. There are three sky-lights high up that have some form, but the big box of the space is very elementary.

My discussions about museums with artists began in the late 1970s, when I was confronted by a group of artists. It was Michael Asher, John Knight, Benjamin Buchloh, and Daniel Buren. They asked, "Okay Mr. Gehry, you love the artist and the work, what kind of museum would you make for us?" And I said what architects have said for a long time and what architects keep saying, "Well, the building is for art, so the art should stand out. The building should be very neutral and should not intrude, it should not in any way compete with the art or become visible. We should be the invisible puppeteer, like in the Japanese dances." I said all of that, and when I finished my holier-than-thou statement I got attacked like I've never been attacked before. I was told, "Goddamnit, you're so stupid. Don't you understand that when we finally get our work to be shown in a museum, we want it to be an important place? If you give us a neutral damn thing it ain't gonna be very important. It's not going to be important in the city, it's not going to have any presence in the community, it's not going to stand up to the courthouse. And when people come, they're going to know that it's the second class, that it's in the background, blah, blah, blah, blah." They really attacked on that basis, and there was a certain sense that it was a very human thing to want your work in a very important place. So I've tried to act on that, I've tried to make rooms that allow for a lot of interaction with the artists, rooms that the artist can manipulate. I've also tried to get rid of all the fussy detail that you find in many new museums, because the fussy detail does, in fact, create problems for the artist.

This is in Barcelona. I didn't intend to make a sculpture. I was asked to make a fish sculpture and I said no, but I did get involved making a trellis over the shopping center, and it ended up looking like a fish. It was very complicated to build and for the first time I used the computer to figure out how to build it. It's a computer system from the French aircraft industry. One of the funny stories about this is that the building behind this is a forty-story Ritz-Carlton Hotel designed by Bruce Graham of SOM. The Ritz-Carlton had one of their people come to look at my model. He kept going way to the back of the model, bending down and taking pictures; he was looking up the back of the trellis. A few days later we got a call from the owner of the project, saying that the Ritz-Carlton man had called. He said they were building this big Ritz-Carlton for fancy guests, people were going to pay a lot of money to stay there, and he didn't want them looking up the asshole of a fish.

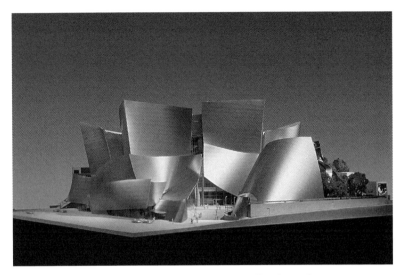

Walt Disney Concert Hall, Los Angeles, California; project 1989.
Final design model.

This is a concert hall in L.A. in the name of Walt Disney, given by the family. I'm not going to get into too much detail about it—it was designed in a collaboration with musical artists. A lot of musicians were involved: members of the Philharmonic Orchestra and a lot of well-known conductors, like Boulez, Rattle and Mehta. Anyone who came to L.A., anyone I could nail down, came in to talk. I wanted it to be festive. The interior was designed kind of like the Berlin Philharmonie by Sharoun in plan; this led to the curved shapes, because acoustically you want the walls concave so that they disburse the sound. It led to sail-like shapes, and then I tried to use this language on the outside.

When you do a building like this you can't show it to the contractor, because they just get very nervous and tell you it's going to cost too much. One thing I've learned from my artist friends is to dig right into the technology, as Richard Serra does with his big

Nationale-Nederlanden Building,
Prague, Czech Republic; 1992/96.

boat hulls and as all artists must do. So we used the computer, and
we made a wall out of the stone we were to use. We had it all digi-
tized with this gadget, so there was a program for each piece of
stone. So we got the sails with an aggregate of the slope, just by the
addition of pieces with a gentle curve to them. The computer gave
us the opportunity to monitor the cost. We had to stay within five
percent double-curved stone, and fifty-fifty single and flat. That
kept us within the budget and this process allowed that.

This is Prague. The town has these nineteenth-century protru-
sions, which I called implied towers. I used the idea of having two
implied towers on the building. This is in a space that had been
accidentally bombed by an American plane in 1945. I started to
make the implied towers, then I heard that the guy next door had
a balcony with a view of the Palace, so I pinched it in. It started to
look like a woman, who I called Ginger, and then this part is Fred.

RECENT WORK

That got back to Czechoslovakia and the press there started saying, "Gehry is bringing Hollywood kitsch to Prague." They really were mad. Havel even gave me a lecture on abstraction, which was quite wonderful. It was actually funny, since I never intended to do what they thought I was doing. But I made an abstract model and showed them what I was doing, and then they were very happy.

As you enter under the building you're walking under the skirts of Ginger, and I sort of liked carrying that metaphor further. The nineteenth-century floor-to-floor was higher; I had a lower floor-to-floor, so I tried to blur the texture of the building, so your eye couldn't run the lines across. I could put a window down at the floor and up at the ceiling, and that gave the floor-to-ceiling height, that's why I did that. And I presumed to add some lines of texture, this was to try and get a kind of a detail that nineteenth-century buildings had, without actually copying them.

Bilbao is a wonderful industrial port, surrounded by beautiful green hills. About thirteen or fourteen years ago, I got a call from Richard Serra, who was in Bilbao. He told me about this tough landscape, this beautiful place he was in; he told me it was very important for me to go and see it. I filed it away, then Tom Krens called me to Bilbao for a meeting about this museum, and that was my first time. I discovered what Serra liked about it. The building is at a bend in the river. They wanted to see the museum from the City Hall so they asked for a tower, which allowed me to figure out a way to embrace this bridge. I thought of Fritz Lang images. I marked a place for Claes and Coosje—my hope at that point was to get them to do the tower—I didn't want to do the tower, as it had no function. I thought, "I'm an architect, I'm not going to do a func-tionless, object kind of thing." So I fought it. The clients—mostly the Basques, but also the Guggenheim—insisted that the tower be part of the architecture. I wasn't supposed to worry about where the artists went. I show this just to show you how I work—I make several scales because it's the only way I can force myself to think of the real building. By forcing myself to go from one scale to the next, I'm forced to think real. If I just work on one size, I sometimes get caught up in just that. Each of the pieces of the building was done in many iterations over a long period of time—it was like watching paint dry. It became like a tailor shop with these patterns. We photographed the result at the end of each day, so that when we went too far, I could go back, two weeks back, and see where we went astray. Then we could catch ourselves up and continue. So these shapes were worked over for a long time.

The computer program was entirely a new one, developed by the Guggenheim and Tom Krens. He wanted a huge gallery without columns, four hundred and some feet long, for changing exhibitions. He wanted a series of classical galleries for dead artists who couldn't defend themselves, and also some galleries that would antagonize the younger artists, to provoke them to either hate it or do something with it. This is because of the history of artists fighting the Frank Lloyd Wright building, which provoked some pretty interesting stuff, and they thought that was positive.

The atrium, when I started it, was very blocky. I thought it was a place to show art. Tom rejected everything I did that was simple. He asked me to do something that was more provocative than the Frank Lloyd Wright building. I got carried away with the images of the idealized cities that architects have drawn for years, but have never been able to realize.

There weren't many pieces of steel in this building that were alike. In this case, the aircraft computer allowed us to precisely measure the steel pieces to seven decimal points of accuracy. So we were able to achieve great savings: the bids actually came in eighteen percent under budget, which is the opposite of what you would think in the normal course of events. Only two very small pieces of steel had to be remade at the end of the project.

The exterior skin was worried over a lot, both in terms of what it did in the light, and also in another whole area of perception

Guggenheim Museum Bilbao, Spain; 1991/97.

that I attribute to my understanding of Bob Irwin's. Originally the metal was going to be stainless steel. I built mock-ups of it, but it looked very cold. What looked good in Minneapolis looked terrible in the Bilbao light. I didn't have many alternatives. We couldn't use lead or copper—copper would be too dark. So I did every god-damned thing you could imagine to stainless steel—I scratched it, embossed it and colored it—but it still looked terrible and I was very dejected. Then I accidentally found a piece of titanium in the files and I pinned it up on the board outside my office. It rained that day by miracle—we had a lot of miracles going on this one—and in the rain the small piece of titanium just glowed. It was beautiful and I knew that that is what we had to get. We found out it was twice the cost of stainless steel, so we couldn't afford it but that's what we had to have. We kept flogging it until we discovered that the titanium could be half the thickness of stainless steel,

Guggenheim Museum Bilbao. Design process model with Perrier bottle, 1992.
Guggenheim Museum Bilbao. Computer-milled model.

therefore it started getting closer to the budget. We had to bid it as an alternate with the stainless. As it was being bid, the Russians dumped a bunch of titanium on the market, and the price came in under the stainless steel. Now once we had it, we gave the sample to the titanium guys to make a prototype. The pieces that came back looked like twenty-year old, dirty, galvanized iron. We then sent one of our people to a titanium mill in Pittsburgh, and he went back and forth every couple of weeks for a year. We discovered that it was like making a salad dressing, it was oil and vinegar—or, in this case, the oil and acids—and once the right combination was poured on the rollers, the titanium took on the look of the sample. It took a year of work to get there.

The nice thing about Bilbao is the industrial character, but the green hills sort of save it. Unfortunately part of this area is now being designed to look like Potomac River Parkway, they're going

RECENT WORK

to sweeten it up and lose the character. There's not much we can do about it. For the tower I used a lot of the stone technology that I developed on the Disney Hall. I tried to make it a gallery of some kind with an elevator, but nobody wanted that; in the end I put a stairway from the bridge that goes down to the riverwalk, but from there up it's nothing.

This is where that stairway comes down from the bridge. I call it my Maurice Chevalier stairway, I can imagine him with his straw hat singing, "I'll build a stairway to paradise." I was willing to do it for the opening but they didn't ask me. I think absorbing this bridge was one of the best things I did, because when you're down there, the traffic passing through is very dynamic.

The bridges and windows face the river, so as you move through the museum, you always return to the center and walk along the river. The river becomes part of the building. The galleries for living artists were designed with catwalks, so that performance art could take place there. That's because it didn't make sense to relegate performance art to a little theatre, especially in terms of what is going on now. I always had the idea that the long gallery would have walls. My friend Tom wouldn't let me put in any walls, and we argue about it to this day. Some people like it this way, but I think it would be better with the walls, as it would give scale to the room.

For the dead artist's galleries we discovered this Spanish ash flooring. The nice thing about it is you get the warmth of the wood, but color doesn't reflect up onto the paintings and it isn't so busy that it interferes.

This is a spec office building complex in Düsseldorf. The buildings took off from the shapes of the binoculars, and I found myself with the problem of the window. Claes and Coosje hid theirs, but I couldn't, so I had to deal with the windows. The windows destroy the sculpture and destroy the form. You probably oughtn't to do things like this, but I finally came up with a window that attacked

Office Complex, Düsseldorf, Germany; 1999. Final design model.
Completed building. Photo highlights unique relations of windows
to the overall geometry of the building.

the building. It went in on a diagonal. I found that if I made one window six thousand times, I could get the price down, and I could turn the window into a texture. There's a good possibility with this, which I wasn't able to completely realize here, but you could aim the windows directionally and create another form that is parallel, or counter, to the form of the building.

This is the Peter Lewis house that I always knew would never be built, or shouldn't be built, or wasn't going to get built. He wasn't going to build it anyway. But it involved bringing in Philip Johnson who did this piece, and Claes and Coosje.

You can see these shapes again come from those shapes of Prague which are similar to the knees, so there is some discussion going on formally between all of us. And the folding and the manipulating of the fold again was giving me courage, from having seen the binoculars built without a lot of difficulty. I was hav-

Lewis Residence, Lyndhurst, Ohio; project 1989/95. Photo features final design with Philip Johnson's octopus-shaped guest house.

ing trouble putting windows in this and Richard Serra one day came in and carved these cracks, and they were so strong and beautiful that I stuck with them.

Out of this came this funny shape that I worked on the computer and loved, but when the house didn't get built I was yearning to do that somewhere. Serra then started playing with those barrel shapes and the cracks, he eventually made what turned into some of the most beautiful sculpture you've all seen. He was only able to do it with the computer guys that were doing my stuff, because as the steel moves through those big rollers it has to change direction every ten or twelve feet, and it could only be done with the computer. So there was this constant back and forth between the technical staff in my office and the artists involved with the project.

 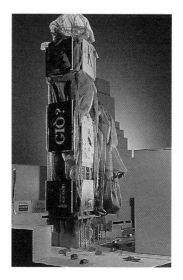

DG Bank Building, Berlin, Germany; 1996/99. Photo highlights conference
center, originally developed for Lewis residence.
One Times Square, New York, New York; project 1996. Final design model.

Claes and Coosje did a bag of sticks for the golf course, because this
site overlooked a golf course. Maggie Keswick Jencks made this run-
nel that she never realized, except in this maquette we made
of it. It was going to run through the site and it was quite beautiful.

I then went to Berlin to work on a competition for a bank. Coin-
cidentally it's the same bank that commissioned Claes and Coosje's
tie sculpture, which they showed earlier. It's the DG Bank in Pariser-
platz. They've built a lot of it back to the way it was in the nineteenth century. The controls on it are horrendous, but we made a
kind of an atrium; and we were able to work within their controls to
develop a facade that was still fairly open. On the back of the building there's an apartment complex, part of which faces the future
Holocaust Memorial. A lot of people have bought these apartments,
although I don't know why there's a run on apartments that face
the Holocaust Memorial. You gotta think about that one.

RECENT WORK

The front was blocky. Judd probably would have liked this one. Inside I made a courtyard in which the offices were all wood, because you can't make a wooden high-rise outside. Inside the space for the competition I tried to make a new shape, but I had trouble. I finally took a previous shape from the Lewis house, and I stuck it in, thinking I'd change it later. We won the competition because of that shape, they loved it, but I don't know why.

This is in Seoul, Korea. The site faces Hyundai. Our client was their enemy, Samsung. We started with a building that had many floors. A lot of floors will work at a place like the Museum of Modern Art in New York, because it's a well-established institution. In a fledgling institution of modern art, we felt that this would inevitably lead to second-class galleries. It's the same issue that Jacques Herzog mentioned in his museum—the attempt to make a sort of equality in the galleries. So we fantasized about what would happen if you floated all the galleries up in the air. The idea finally resolved itself in a square spiral that started about sixty feet in the ground. There's a large gallery at ground level. All of the galleries had top light, which solved the concern I had about second-class galleries. What worried me was that if there were second-class galleries, the Korean artists would end up there, this usually happens in an international art scene, and it gives the wrong message. I was interested in imagery, and nothing in Seoul interested me more than the landscape. The built environment since the war is pretty horrendous, so I started to explore the issues of nature and landscape, and how to bring that into the building.

This is a section showing the big gallery downstairs, you would be able to look in from the street level. The galleries then step up, and the problem was how to get a sense of continuity, because the spaces go up and down. The client asked for only rectilinear galleries. They're in there, the space between the curved outside wall and the rectilinear gallery is the space for the escalators and stairways, so you are always traveling in a space that has some

Weatherhead School of Management, Case Western Reserve University,
Cleveland, Ohio; project 1998. Final design model.
Samsung Museum of Modern Art, Seoul, Korea; project 1995.
Final design model.

form, then you arrive into a rectilinear space. Midway through the
design of the project, we were informed that a nearby building
could not be purchased. That stopped the project, and I think it's
now a dead duck. This came after Bilbao, I was interested in trying
to get a kind of waterfall feeling, a feeling of nature. I didn't
particularly like the flaps on the building and with time I would
have fixed them. This picture is my favorite because it starts to
have a liquid character, something that I got here for the first
time. Anyway, it's painful when you work several years on something like this, then you get there and it's beyond your control.

Here's the business school at Case Western. The metal parts are
the classrooms. If I went into detail I could prove to you that all of
the exterior shapes are represented inside, that the rooms are
close to the skin, and that there is no wasted space. It's not like
what it looks like, but I'm not going explain it. Trust me.

Because Jacques showed his building, I thought I'd show this collaboration between Richard Serra, myself, and Jorg Schlaich. It's for the footbridge between St. Paul's and the Tate Bankside. We didn't win, we had a scheme that would have won, but being who we are, we couldn't change our stripes. You want to say, "Look, we can just do a footbridge and that's fine, but can't we bring a little more to the table, because of what we do?" We were fascinated with the volume of the dome and the volume of the large building. We tried to develop an object that would have its own character, we wanted more than a laid-back piece that wouldn't take these guys on. We tried to make a form that sort of speaks to both structures. The bridge that was chosen just comes straight across, it doesn't really deal with the relationship to the building. We didn't want to plop down on this plaza, so we made an overlook where people could enjoy the art from above. But we lost. And we're not mad either, we're happy.

This, finally, is where the chainlink went. I've shown it to Irwin more than anybody, Time Warner rented this building in New York. They've got all this stuff on it that pays for the building, so the interiors are a wasteland: they're void, empty, and can't be rented. They don't want to rent them, they make enough money on the outside. Time Warner wants to put a store at the bottom and a little restaurant/bar up at the top. They asked us if we could do something to this building that would contain all of the ads, yet give it an identity as a separate image. They want to say that it's the Time Warner Building, instead of just a thing with all these billboards on it. I struggled with it a lot, I didn't think we could do it. First I said no, I couldn't do it. I didn't see how you *could* do it. And I found out that zoning would only allow a projection of three feet, and three feet in this mess isn't going to help you at all. But then I talked to one of the fancy zoning lawyers. He suggested I might get away with it if I could figure out a way to project out, then bring it back in every once in a while. I got fixed on the idea of a cuckoo clock, because Time Warner owns all these figures like Bugs Bunny, Superman, and Batman. I thought it would be great if one of those figures came out every hour. So we found a wonderful mesh, not chainlink, it's a fancy, woven fabric. We could have covered the building with it, and it could pull up its skirts and show you all its stuff on the inside. So we would hide all the figures behind the mesh and then at noon, Superman could pull the curtain and come flying out. Well, they loved it. They told me I was a real genius, they danced around the model, and they left with all the pictures, and I never heard from them again.

This is Modena, Italy. They are going to celebrate the fact that four hundred years ago, the Duke D'Este returned here with his collection from Ferrara. Jim Ackerman could probably explain this better than I can. I was dragged there by a bunch of art historian types to meet the mayor. They wanted something architectural, a gateway for the city. I got pretty excited because Modena's a pretty wonderful place. The square used to have a gate, it's now filled with tramlines and all kinds of stuff. I met with the mayor, who really wanted me to do this. I asked him what the budget was and he said one million dollars. I said one million dollars doesn't buy you nothing—you know, a few plane fares over here and you've used it all up. I ain't gonna stay in El Paisano hotel in Modena. So I negotiated a fee and a deal, and I said okay, it's going to cost you $100,000 for me to move. He said fine, and I said okay. The idea is I'm going to get three big construction cranes and hang all this *schmatta* stuff on it and project images. The guy was in shock for a little while. Then we found three cranes that have now been donated to the city, and we're going to get that metal and we're going project images. So that's the idea.

Millennium Bridge Competition, London, England; competition 1996.
Final design model. Joint project with Richard Serra and Jorg Schlaich.

CONTRIBUTORS

JAMES S. ACKERMAN

After receiving his B.A. and M.A. from Yale University, New Haven, Connecticut, James Ackerman went on to complete his Ph.D. at New York University. Early in his career Ackerman received a Fulbright Fellowship and the 25th Anniversary Medal of the National Gallery of Art for distinguished service to art education. He joined Harvard University, Cambridge, Massachusetts in 1961 where he is now the Arthur Kingsley Porter Professor of Arts, Emeritus. Over the last thirty years he has held many visiting teaching positions including Slade Professor of Fine Art, University of Cambridge, England; Meyer Shapiro Visiting Professor of Art History, Columbia University, New York, New York; Visiting Professor of Fine Arts, N.Y.U. Institute of Fine Arts, New York; and Visiting Professor of Architecture, M.I.T., Cambridge. While continually publishing essays and articles on the history of architecture with critical and historical theory, Ackerman has also published a number of writings on Renaissance architecture and has worked on several films focusing on architecture.

James Ackerman holds honorary degrees from Kenyon College, Gambier, Ohio; the University of Maryland, College Park; and the Massachusetts College of Art, Boston. He is a fellow of the American Academy of Arts and Sciences and a Fellow and Trustee of the American Academy in Rome, Italy. Ackerman has also been decorated as the Grand Officer in the Order of Merit of the Italian Republic. He is the author of many studies on Italian architecture, including *The Cortile del Belvedere* (1954) and *The Architecture of Michelangelo* (1961). Other books include *The Villa: Form and Ideology of Country Houses* (1990), a collection of essays entitled *Distance Points* (1992), and *Palladio the Architect and His Influence in America* (1980).

MICHAEL A. BENEDIKT

Michael Benedikt is the Harwell Hamilton Harris Regents Professor of Architecture and the Director of the Center for American Architecture and Design at the University Texas at Austin, where he has taught design studio and design theory since 1975. He is a graduate of the University of the Witwatersrand, South Africa and of Yale University, New Haven, Connecticut. Benedikt has practiced architecture both in medium-sized firms and on his own, with a number of buildings to his credit in Austin. His books include *For an Architecture of Reality* (1987), *Deconstructing the Kimbell* (1991), both in their fourth printing, and *Cyberspace: First Steps*, now in its eighth printing and translated into four languages. He is also the executive editor of the journal *CENTER: Architecture and Design in America*.

Widely regarded as one of the founders of today's cyberspace/VR theory movement, Benedikt has organized several international conferences on the topic. He has published over fifty articles and book reviews, and has delivered over eighty invited lectures in the U.S. and abroad on architecture, design theory, computers, social trends, art and ethics.

FRANK O. GEHRY

Frank Gehry received his architecture degree from the University of Southern California, Los Angeles, and also studied City Planning at Harvard University Graduate School of Design, Cambridge, Massachusetts. He has been bestowed honorary doctoral degrees from the Rhode Island School of Design, Providence; the California Institute of the Arts, Valencia; the Southern California Institute of Architecture, Los Angeles; and Parsons School of Design, New York, New York. Gehry has held a Professorship at Yale University, New Haven, Connecticut, and the Eliot Noyes Chair at Harvard.

Gehry's architectural firm, Frank O. Gehry and Associates, was established in 1962. It has grown significantly over time, with international museum, theater, performance, institutional, commercial, and residential projects. A recent endeavor, and perhaps one of the most publicized and acclaimed, is the Guggenheim Museum, Bilbao, Spain, completed in 1997. Other significant projects include the Samsung Museum of Contemporary Art, Seoul, Korea; the American Center, Paris, France; the EuroDisney Retail and Entertainment Center outside of Paris; the Frederick R. Weisman Art Museum, Minneapolis, Minnesota; and the Chiat/Day Building, Venice, California, a collaboration with Claes Oldenburg and Coosje van Bruggen.

Over the past three decades, Gehry has earned several of the most distinguished awards in the architectural field. He was awarded the Pritzker Architecture Prize in 1989, and received the Praemium Imperiale Award by the Japan Art Association in 1992. Gehry has received over one hundred national and regional American Institute of Architecture awards for his work and was elected to its College of Fellows in 1974.

JACQUES HERZOG & PIERRE DE MEURON

Jacques Herzog and Pierre de Meuron have become recognized as two of the most inventive and skillful architects working today. They have built cultural, commercial, and institutional buildings, and were chosen out of 150 competing architectural firms to design the Tate Modern, London, England.

Herzog and de Meuron have been in partnership since 1978. Both architects were awarded their degree in architecture from the ETH Zürich, Switzerland, and both have been visiting professors at Harvard University, Cambridge, Massachusetts, in 1989, 1994, 1996, and 1998. They have completed over one hundred projects, including the storage building for Ricola, Laufen, Switzerland; the Library and Seminar Buildings for the Eberswalde Technical School, Germany; and a gallery for the Goetz Collection, Munich, Germany. They are currently working on ten planned constructions including museums and commercial buildings in France, Germany, and Switzerland. Herzog and de Meuron were among the three firms short-listed for the expansion of the Museum of Modern Art, New York, New York. The Dominus Winery in Napa Valley, California was their first realized project in the United States.

RONI HORN

Roni Horn received her M.F.A. at Yale University, New Haven, Connecticut, where she is now a visiting professor. Her work has been exhibited in galleries and museums throughout the world. Major exhibitions include *You Are the Weather*, Fotomuseum Winterthur, Switzerland; *Earth Grows Thick*, Wexner Center for the Arts, Columbus, Ohio;

Making Being Here Enough, Kunsthalle Basel, Switzerland; *Inner Geography*, Baltimore Museum of Art, Maryland; and *Rare Spellings*, Kunstmuseum Winterthur, Switzerland. Other one–person museum exhibitions include the Museum of Contemporary Art, Los Angeles, California; the Detroit Institute of Arts, Illinois; the Neuberger Museum, Purchase, New York; and Yale University. Roni Horn's work has been selected for prestigious survey exhibitions of contemporary art including the 1997 Venice Biennale, Italy; Documenta IX, Kassel, Germany; and the 1991 Whitney Biennial, New York, New York.

Roni Horn has been awarded numerous grants and fellowships including a Guggenheim Fellowship, three NEA Fellowships and the 1998 CalArts award in Fine Arts. She recently completed a permanent installation at Bahnhof Ost, Basel. Her work *Things That Happen Again* has been on view at the Chinati Foundation since 1988.

ROBERT IRWIN

Robert Irwin attended Dorsey High School, Los Angeles, California from 1943 to 1946 and subsequently attended the Otis Art Institute, the Jepson Art Institute, and the Chouinard Art Institute, all in Los Angeles. In 1979 he received an Honorary Doctorate in Art from the

San Francisco Art Institute, California. Beginning in 1970, Irwin's teaching took the peripatetic form of accepting invitations to lecture or participate in symposia and seminars with students and professionals. He has visited over 150 universities and art institutes in forty states, speaking on topics relating to art, architecture, philosophy, and perceptual psychology.

Irwin's work has been exhibited in galleries and museums since the mid-1950s, and is in the permanent collections of the Denver Art Museum, Colorado; Museum of Contemporary Art, Los Angeles, California; the J. Paul Getty Center, Los Angeles; Museo Nacional Centro de Arte Reina Sofia, Madrid, Spain; The Museum of Modern Art, New York, New York; and the Walker Art Center, Minneapolis, Minnesota. A retrospective of Irwin's work was organized by the Museum of Contemporary Art, Los Angeles in 1993 and subsequently traveled to museums in Cologne, Paris, Madrid, and New York. Since 1970, Irwin's works are created only in relation to specific landscapes or architectural situations. Permanently installed works include *Portal Park Slice*, Dallas, Texas; *Fifty-six Shadow Planes*, the Old Post Office Atrium, Washington, D.C.; and Two *Violet V Forms*, University of California, San Diego. His garden at the J. Paul Getty Center was completed in 1997. An installation at the Dia Center for the Arts, New York, New York, opened in April 1998.

CLAES OLDENBURG & COOSJE VAN BRUGGEN

Claes Oldenburg studied at Yale University, New Haven, Connecticut and at the Art Institute of Chicago, Illinois, and has lived in New York, New York since 1956. His work has been shown in solo gallery exhibitions since 1959, and has been the subject of numerous museum exhibitions in the United States and abroad. An extensive retrospective of his work, *Claes Oldenburg: An Anthology*, was organized in 1995 by the National Gallery of Art, Washington, D.C., and traveled to several museums in the United States, Germany, and England. Oldenburg is represented in the permanent collections of major international museums including the Art Gallery of Ontario, Toronto, Canada; The Art Institute of Chicago; the Solomon R. Guggenheim Museum, New York; the Museum of Contemporary Art, Los Angeles, California; the Museum of Modern Art, New York, New York; the National Gallery of Art, Washington; the Stedelijk Museum, Amsterdam, The Netherlands; and the Tate Gallery, London, England.

Coosje van Bruggen received a Ph.D. in Art History from the University of Groningen, The Netherlands. From 1967 to 1971 she was a curator at the Stedelijk Museum, and from 1971 to 1976 she taught at the Academy of Fine Arts in Enschede, The Netherlands. In 1982 she was a member of the selection committee for

Documenta VII, Kassel, Germany. She conceived the characters for and was a co-author of *Il Corso del Coltello*, with Claes Oldenburg and Frank O. Gehry, performed in Venice, Italy in 1985. Coosje van Bruggen is the author of *Claes Oldenburg; Mouse Museum/Ray Gun Wing* ; *"The Realistic Imagination and Imaginary Reality of Claes Oldenburg"* in *Claes Oldenburg: Drawings 1959–1989*; *Claes Oldenburg: Just Another Room*; *Bruce Nauman*; and *John Baldessari*. In 1991 she curated a limited edition artist book by Hanne Darboven *Urzeit/Urzeit*.

Oldenburg and van Bruggen were married in 1976 and have collaborated on numerous large-scale public projects and performances including *Flashlight*, Las Vegas, Nevada; *Spoonbridge and Cherry*, Walker Art Center, Minneapolis, Minnesota; *Free Stamp*, Cleveland, Ohio; and *Shuttlecocks*, Nelson–Atkins Museum, Kansas City, Missouri. Their *Monument to the Last Horse* was created for the Chinati Foundation in 1991.

tions of noteworthy houses and commercial structures, interior design, custom furniture design, and garden design. William Stern recently completed the renovation and expansion of the Contemporary Art Museum, Houston. His firm has received numerous awards from the Texas Society of Architects and the Houston Chapter of the American Institute of Architects.

The work of Stern & Bucek Architects has been published in several books and journals including *Texas Architect*, *The Architecture Review*, *Architecture*, *Metropolitan Home*, *Esquire*, and others. Stern is currently an Adjunct Associate Professor at the University of Houston's College of Architecture where he teaches undergraduate design studios as well as seminar courses on the history of American architecture. He is on the executive board of the Rice Design Alliance, Houston, and is a founding editor and frequent contributor to its publication, *Cite: The Architecture and Design Review of Houston*.

WILLIAM F. STERN

William Stern received his Master of Architecture degree at Harvard University's Graduate School of Design, Cambridge, Massachusetts. After moving to Houston, Texas in 1974, he formed his own practice there in 1979. The work of Stern & Bucek Architects varies from single family to multi–family housing, restora-

ACKNOWLEDGEMENTS

Sterry Butcher
Kelly McRaven
City of Marfa
Marfa Independent School District
Sul Ross State University

Funding for the *Art and Architecture* symposium and accompanying publication was provided by the following individuals and foundations:

The Burkitt Foundation
The Brown Foundation
Andrew Cogan
Lynn and Tim Crowley
Maxine and Stuart Frankel
Agnes Gund
Maureen and John Jerome
Michael and Jeannie Klein
Annalee Newman
George and Frances Reid
Deedie and Rusty Rose
Martha Stewart
Still Water Foundation

PHOTO CREDITS

©Becky Cohen: pages 100, 107
©Todd Eberle: pages 71, 152
Courtesy Frank Gehry Studio:
    pages 161-181
Courtesy Peggy Guggenheim
    Museum: page 21
©Hayes-Davidson: pages 49, 50 right
©Herzog & de Meuron: pages 33, 34,
    39 right, 43, 50 left, 51-57
Courtesy Roni Horn:
    pages 60-69, 77, 78
Courtesy Robert Irwin:
    pages 88-99, 103
Courtesy Donald Judd Foundation,
    licensed by VAGA: pages 25, 26
©Jannes Linders, courtesy Jablonka
    Galerie: page 73
Courtesy Claes Oldenburg
    and Coosje van Bruggen:
    pages 126-149, 153-157
©Christian Richters: page 42
©Thomas Ruff: pages 35, 37, 45
©Ulrich Schwarz: page 39 left
Courtesy Richard Serra: pages 27, 29
©Margherita Spiluttini: page 47

COLOPHON

Art and Architecture was edited by
Jeffrey Kopie. The graphic design
is by Rutger Fuchs, Amsterdam.
The text, typeset in *Swift* (1985) by
Gerard Unger, was printed in the
United States by Becotte & Company
in Philadelphia, Pennsylvania.